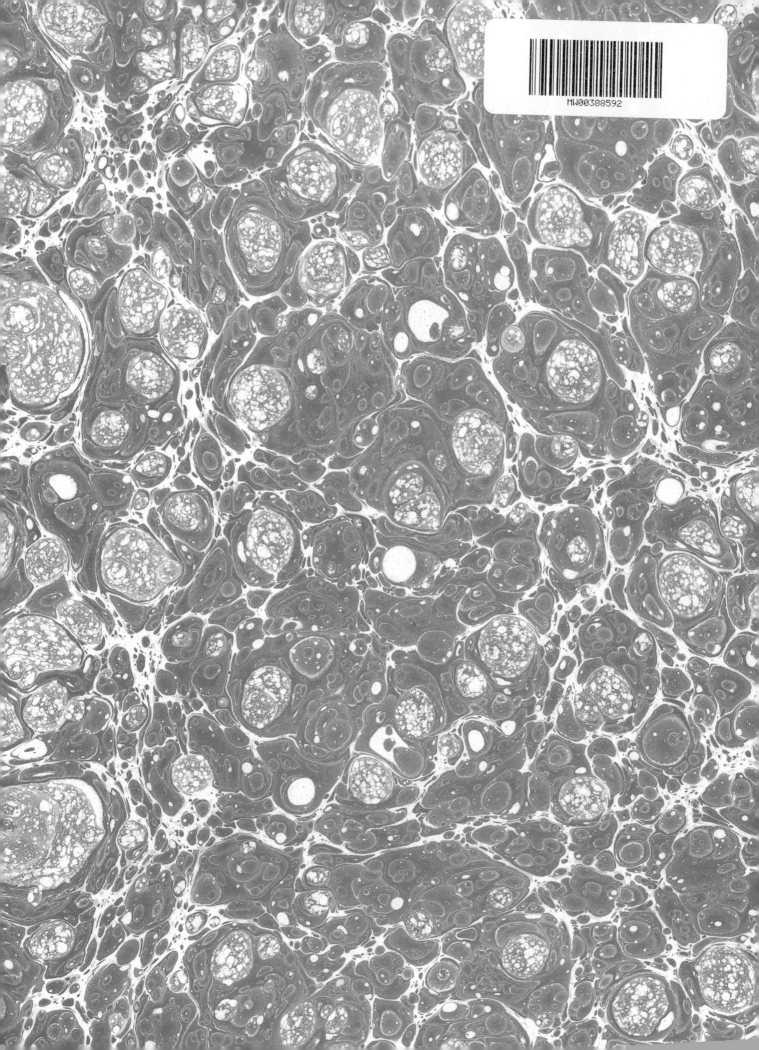

COWBOY EQUIPMENT

JOICE OVERTON

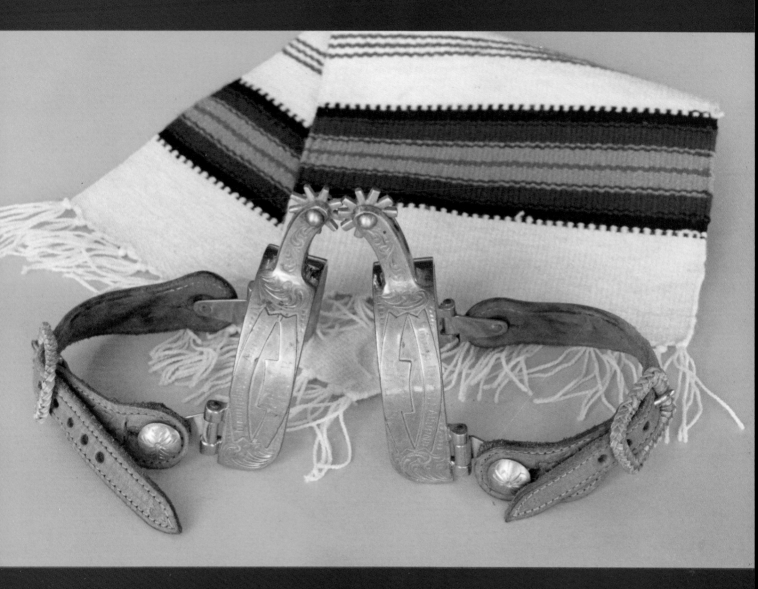

Schiffer Publishing Ltd

4880 Lower Valley Road, Atglen, PA 19310 USA

This book is dedicated to all of my family members, who each hold a very precious place in my heart. During the course of this writing I lost my Mother, Leona McGinness Hunsucker, 1917-1997, to her it is especially dedicated.

The other dearly loved family members consist of: Bill Overton, my husband; Lance Rider, son; Sonny Rider, son; Paul Rider, son; Frank Hunsucker, brother; Babe Turvey, sister.

And now, more than ever, it is dedicated to God, who " …girdeth me with strength." Psalm 18:32

Library of Congress Cataloging-in-Publication Data

Overton, Joice I.
  Cowboy equipment/Joice Overton.
    p. cm.
  Includes bibliographical references and index.
  ISBN 0-7643-0405-4
    1. Cowboys--Collectibles--West (U.S.)--Catalogs.
  2. Frontier and pioneer life--West (U.S.)--Collectibles-
  -Catalogs. 3. Cattle trade--West (U.S.)--Equipment and
  supplies--Collectors and collecting--Catalogs. I. Title.
  F596.0944 1997
  978--dc21   97-29686
              CIP

Designed by "Sue"

ISBN: 0-7643-0405-4
Printed in China
1 2 3 4

Published by Schiffer Publishing Ltd.
4880 Lower Valley Road
Atglen, PA 19310
Phone: (610) 593-1777; Fax: (610) 593-2002
E-mail: Schifferbk@aol.com

Please write for a free catalog.
This book may be purchased from the publisher.
Please include $3.95 for shipping.

Please try your bookstore first.

We are interested in hearing from authors
with book ideas on related subjects.

CONTENTS

ACKNOWLEDGMENTS

I would like to say a sincere and heartfelt "Thank You" to my friends who have allowed me to photograph their collections:

To Paul and Marlene Snider, "Collectors Extraordinare" and certainly the finest folks it has ever been my privilege to know. They have more than once "pulled my bacon out of the fire," and I will always be especially grateful to them.

To Jack Snider (thanks again Jack).

To Bob and Judy Bertsch.

To Larry and Aileen Fisher, friends and neighbors we have enjoyed for over twenty years now.

To Marlin Pool, a true cowboy at heart.

To Mark Loge Nelson, Author of *Bibliography of Old Time Saddlemakers* (the address for his book is found in the *Bibliography*).

To Phyllis A. Shovelski.

To Roy and Jeanenne Williams.

To William Scott Deatherage.

To Alyce Jennings Anderson.

To Orville Sears Jr.

To Don Rock.

And a very special Thank You to Ken Williams at Computer Processing Unlimited, Hermiston, Oregon.

Without the kind help and generosity of each one, this book would not have been possible.

PREFACE

The Western cowboy has been a part of the American scene for a very long time. One of the most amusing pieces of literary work I have ever read was published in 1872, and was so apropos to the cowboy life, it may well have been written and published in 1972 and none would have been the wiser.

It was written by Mark Twain.

It seems that he was in Carson, Nevada, and was very much impressed with the Western cowboy style of riding and with the horses there. He attended a horse auction and in his words:

"I was resolved to buy a horse…A man whom I did not know (he turned out to be the auctioneer's brother) noticed a wistful look in my eye and observed that that was a very remarkable horse to be going at such a price; and added that the saddle alone was worth the money. It was a Spanish saddle with ponderous tapideros, and furnished with un-gainly sole leather covering with the unspellable name.

"I said I had half a notion to bid. Then this keen-eyed person appeared to me to be taking my measure; but I dismissed the suspicion when he spoke, for his manner was full of guileless candor and truthfulness. Said he; I know that horse, know him well. You are a stranger, I take it, and so you might think he was an American horse, maybe, but I assure you he is not. He is nothing of the kind; but…excuse my speaking in a low voice, other people being near…he is, without the shadow of a doubt, a Genuine Mexican Plug!

"I did not know what a Genuine Mexican Plug was, but there was something about this mans way of saying it, that made me swear inwardly that I would own a Genuine Mexican Plug, or die!"

Mark Twain ends his short story with: "In the afternoon I brought the creature into the plaza, and certain citizens held him by the head, and others by the tail, while I mounted him."

He goes on to say: "The third time I went up I heard a stranger say…Oh don't he buck though! While I was up, somebody struck the horse a sounding thwack with a leathern strap, and when I arrived again, the Genuine Mexican Plug was not there."

Excerpt from "Roughing It," published 1872.

This book is about collecting the colorful cowboy equipment that men were using and wearing in the story Mark Twain wrote about.

Some of these items have been carefully preserved, others show hard use and some deterioration. Some could probably tell many wild and exciting tales if they could only speak. I have tried to be completely accurate in each description, and beg your forgiveness wherever I may have failed.

INTRODUCTION

It may seem strange to begin this book by noting an analogy to the tomb of Tutankhamen, but it has been in my mind so many times as I repeatedly viewed and photographed these beautiful cowboy items.

On November 26, 1922, a man named Howard Carter viewed for the very first time the items within the tomb through a small "peep-hole" he had just drilled in a wall. When asked what he could see, he replied: "Wonderful Things." In the summer and fall of 1996, as I looked through the "peep-hole" of my cameras, that particular description came to my mind many times as I photographed all of these "Wonderful Things."

While it is true that the cowboy equipment featured in this book has not been hidden away for over 3,000 years, as were Tutankhamen's, there is still a parallel to be found, for each represent a way of life that has passed out of existence forever. Collecting items such as these is sometimes seen as a chance to make the past live again, therefore, they become "treasure."

As collectors of the Western cowboy equipment will tell you, every piece is rare and scarce, as they doggedly pursue them in every part of the country. They are sought after at almost every level of possible obtainment. From yard sales to auctions, from thrift stores to antique shops, they are being hunted today, but efforts, sadly enough, have been yielding less and less as these items find their way into the hands of collectors who simply hold onto them. Some are finding their way into foreign collections around the world now, and are therefore lost to us forever.

Why do we seek these items in the first place? Is it perhaps that we are realizing a way of life is passing into obscurity right before our very eyes here in America? These items of equipment used by the Western cowboy are simple reminders of a unique way of life and livelihood in America, the remnants of a special time and era. We all try to hold onto it, for none of us wish to see the end of the Western cowboy, but in our hearts we know it has come. We know that in most cases, technology today has replaced the cowboy, the ATV is the "horse" on many cattle ranches...the eighteen-wheel cattle hauling truck is the "Ram Rod," its driver the "Trail Boss," and we are finding that the rare almost extinct "breed" called "cowboy" is found more and more at rodeos only.

So it is with a fondness for all that it ever represented, for all that it stood for and meant, that we lovingly collect and treasure what seems at times all we have left; the cowboy Equipment.

I hope you will enjoy seeing some of the "tools of his trade," as much as I enjoyed putting them on film and in this book, for they were truly; "Wonderful Things."

CHAPTER ONE
SADDLES

"Saddle Strings"

"Saddle strings, insignificant things...
Just strips of oiled deerhide;
But their pull is strong
And their hold is long
On the years when you used to ride.

Saddle strings!, an old heart sings
Of days when the west was wide,
And sighs. Perhaps
To those saddle flaps
A bit of his heart is tied."

—Don Rognon

It is a proven fact that Julius Caesar wrote of saddles! Sculptures contemporary to that time frame have confirmed this. The use of the saddle can be dated back as far as the 5th century B.C., with its earliest form being a simple cloth between rider and horse. Some of these cloths were anchored with "breast collar" and "cinch," some were not. It is believed that saddles with frames were also in use as far back as the 4th and 5th centuries B.C.

As with so many other things in the realm of cowboy gear, our own Western Saddle as we know it today had its beginning with the advent of the Conquistadors. We know that the saddles brought to the Western Hemisphere in the sixteenth century were Spanish War Saddles. They were basically designed with one main purpose in mind; that of keeping the rider on the horse after being hit with hard thrusts of war lances and other weapons. Naturally, they were a form of "wrap-around" with front high swells, no horn, and high backed cantles. Stirrups were sometimes used, and sometimes not, depending on whether or not they were to be used with armor on.

The evolution of the saddle continued as the Spanish settled in Mexico and began to expand colonies and missions into what is now America. The Mexican Vaquero saddle was developed for working cattle in the new open country of the colonized Americas and was quite a variation from the earlier Spanish War saddle. They were hide covered trees, lower cantles with wooden stirrups, and no saddle horn. Later on in the 1860s a large flat round horn was added as the use of the lariat became prevalent for the handling of cattle. Some of these early Vaquero saddles were a nightmare of wooden devices that were surely torture to both rider and animal.

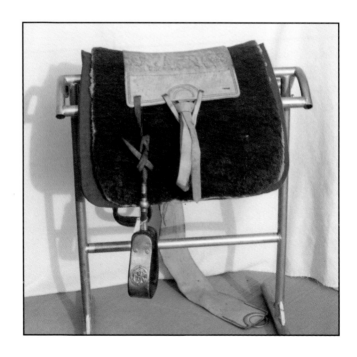

First layer, with leather pad and stirrups, of Argentine multi-layered saddle. *Courtesy Paul and Marlene Snider.*

Then, as history has it, Daniel Boone opened up the way West of the Alleghenies and after 1770 Americans rode West on flat English style saddles. The early English saddles were leather with low cantles and no saddle horn, generally with stirrups hanging from narrow leathers, but not fenders. Many were in use all during our frontier period.

Progress in the development of the saddle seemed to almost "explode" into new innovations by the early 1800s. Tapideros, horns, center fire rigging, the layered saddle

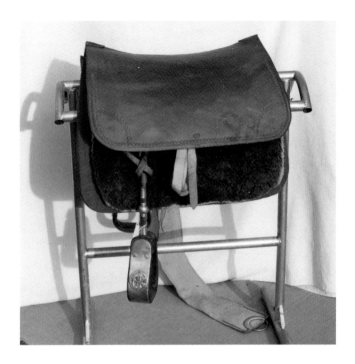

Second layer of multi-layered saddle, the leather piece is border tooled and very thick cowhide. *Courtesy Paul and Marlene Snider.*

with mochila (or covering over the tree), and the list goes on. By 1859 the McClellan entered the scene as the accepted Military saddle, and in 1860 the Mother Hubbard had been made, and was a front runner for saddles with fixed or attached mochila or coverings over the tree. Stirrups varied from wooden to occasional iron rings.

Texas cowboys used a variety of old early Mother Hubbards and Vaquero types to drive cattle and sheep north. After the Civil War, double rigged saddles began to appear on Texas saddles, and the mochila had begun to evolve into the square skirted saddle of Texas fame. However, some square mochilas were still being used during the pony-express time. By the 1880s, the saddle making trade had blossomed into one of the most lucrative industries in the country.

As with so many other pieces of equipment the cowboy used, "necessity was truly the mother of invention." If he needed something to tie off a lariat to, the horn was invented, when he needed protection from the animal's sweat, the fenders were invented, and the cowboy himself was always the director of the innovation. It is interesting to note that one of the few things added for ornamentation only was the "Cheyenne Roll," which is a simple rolled under edge to the cantle. But, even then, it also had some use in the long run, as I can personally testify to, for it sure makes a handy "hold on" when you get into trouble!

There are three basic kinds of rigging in saddles. The first is the double rig, or a saddle equipped with two cinch rings on each side, and intended for a front and rear cinch. The three quarter rig is where the cinch ring is held by a

long strap and a short one so the cinch girths the horse a few inches behind his front legs. And finally the center fire rig is the one in which the cinch ring drops directly under the stirrups.

While the Texans seemed to prefer the square skirted saddle, the Californians developed the round skirt that was, and still is, popular today.

The cowboy world in the late 1800s saw a saddle shop in almost every town. Saddle making and saddle repairing was in full bloom. Saddles began to be "regionized" as to identification and names, i.e.: "The Pocatello," "The Casper," "The Cheyenne," "The Colorado," "The Green River," "The Prescott," and so on.

There was no single piece of working equipment more important to a cowboy than his saddle. Often times the early big ranches furnished a man the horse, but seldom his saddle. A cowboy's saddle was his ultimate working tool—sometimes in its seat from daylight until dark, and even then using it for his pillow at night. It became a simple matter of fact that when it was said a man had "sold the saddle," it was understood that he was done for. Another old cowboy saying that's been around for quite awhile is: "Every man in his lifetime is due, one good woman, one good horse, and one good saddle," the connotation being that each were good for one lifetime!

Sometimes a man had kept and used his saddle for forty years or more, as the life of a well-built saddle was almost equal to that of a man's working years. I have seen many saddles that were fifty or sixty years old and are just as safe to use today as were when they were built. One sits in my own barn today and has been in our fam-

Third layer of multi-layered saddle. This piece is hand tooled and has padded leather "bars" that run the length of it with beautiful large flat medallions in front piece that are silver and gold. *Courtesy Paul and Marlene Snider.*

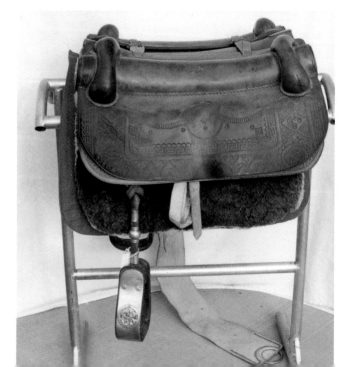

ily since the day it was made and was presented to Mr. Overton as a trophy saddle in 1948. It is in wonderful condition yet.

Strange as it may seem, there are some serious saddlemakers today who are returning to some of the earlier styles. The Pullman Saddle Company in New Palestine, Indiana, is currently offering two beautiful old styles, one with a round skirt and one square skirted. Both feature full Tapideros, high cantles, slick seats, and the old fashioned fenders. So there could be a trend in saddle making today to return to the old "yesterday basics" for style, and for the actual working cowboys around the country, this has to be a big plus!

When it comes to saddle care, the best thing you can do to protect and preserve an old saddle is to keep it in a dry place, with moth ball protection for the sheep skin lining, if it has it. Some occasional wiping down with a very good liquid glycerin saddle soap, applied with a piece of sheep skin is good. As a final step, rub it down well with Neatsfoot Oil on a soft cloth. This is your best bet for good preservation, and appearance. Never use water of any kind on a saddle, and never, ever use vegetable oils or motor oils, no matter what anyone tells you. If you use these methods, your saddle may look just fine for a while, but in the long haul you will be sorry. With good care, the saddles that you have or collect are very long-term items and will last for many many years.

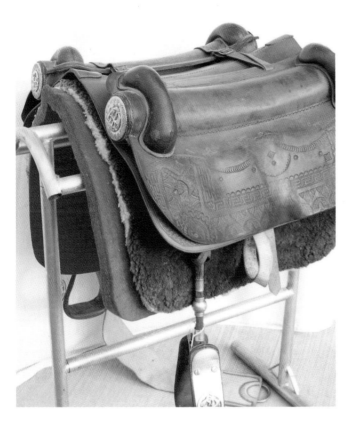

Third layer showing silver and gold medallions in front. *Courtesy Paul and Marlene Snider.*

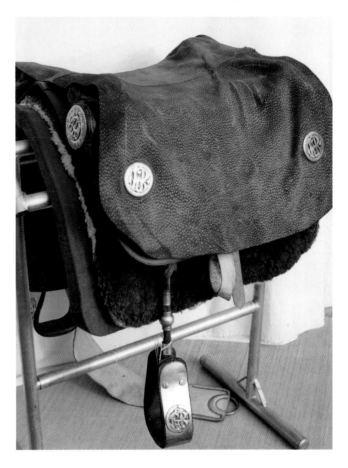

Fourth layer of multi-layered saddle. This piece is a soft suede leather covering that bears the same matching medallions of silver and gold. The saddle is now complete. *Courtesy Paul and Marlene Snider.* $6000.

Detail of silver and gold medallion on multi-layered saddle. *Courtesy Paul and Marlene Snider.*

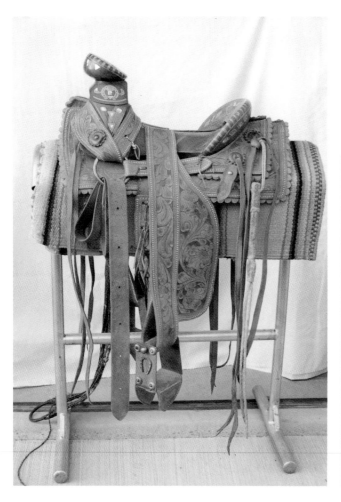

Very ornate charro saddle c. 1930, with fancy mother-of-pearl inlays, fancy corded cinch. It is built on a wooden frame. Marked "L.A. Moderna" as maker. *Courtesy Paul and Marlene Snider.* $1000-1200.

Detail of mother-of-pearl inlay on saddle horn of charro saddle. *Courtesy Paul and Marlene Snider.*

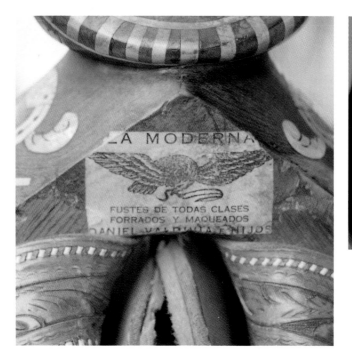

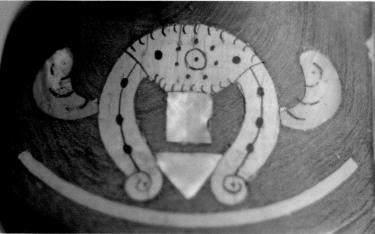

Mother-of-pearl detail on previous charro saddle. *Courtesy Paul and Marlene Snider.*

Makers mark on charro saddle. *Courtesy Paul and Marlene Snider.*

This ancient Native American saddle was captured from white men by members of the Sioux tribe, whereby they removed all of the leather covering from the Army Issue saddle tree, (a McClellan), and then added the metal headed tacks later, c. 1860-1875. *Courtesy Paul and Marlene Snider.* $950-1150

Squaw saddle, Nez Perce, made from rawhide and elk antler, the saddle bears one of the crudest saddle marks: "Made By Thayts-1880". *Courtesy Paul and Marlene Snider.* $600-800

Very old "sawbuck" packer saddle, this was used by early "Mountain Men". *Courtesy Paul and Marlene Snider.* $60-75

Unique and quite old Mexican made saddle from mesquite wood with an unusual "knot" horn. *Courtesy Paul and Marlene Snider.* $300-400

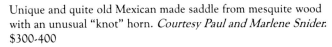

Rawhide Native American saddle with elk antler forks, cottonwood bars. *Courtesy Paul and Marlene Snider.* $500-600

Rawhide Native American made, this saddle has seen lots of years and lots of weather, but is still a great piece of history. *Courtesy Paul and Marlene Snider.* $500-600

Lovely old Native American Squaw saddle, with bead work and white deerskin. *Courtesy Paul and Marlene Snider.* $4000-5000

Old rawhide Squaw saddle with high horn and bone forks. *Courtesy Paul and Marlene Snider.* $500-600

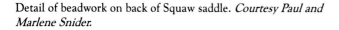

Detail of beadwork on back of Squaw saddle. *Courtesy Paul and Marlene Snider.*

Detail of beaded Squaw saddle, showing little "sheep bell" in front and hanging beads from the saddle horn. *Courtesy Paul and Marlene Snider.*

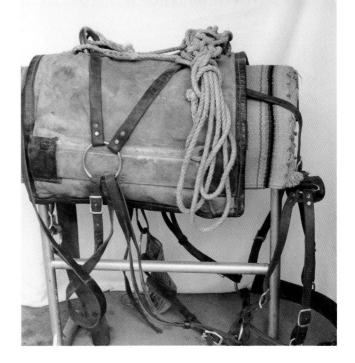

Packer saddle "Decker" designed this famous packer, at Kooskia, Idaho, as they packed into the great Clearwater Country. O.P. Robinette is the maker of this model. *Courtesy Paul and Marlene Snider.* $350-450

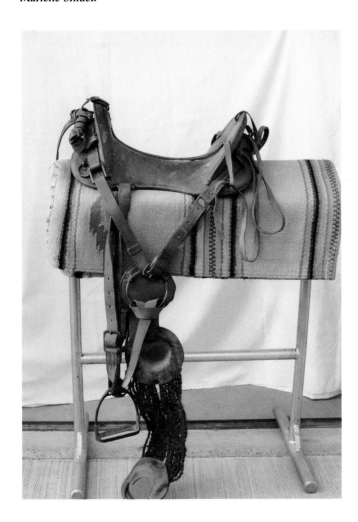

U.S. Cavalry, McClellan saddle, c. 1917, in pristine condition with the original horse hair strap and cinch. This is an original Military issue. *Courtesy Paul and Marlene Snider.* $800-1000

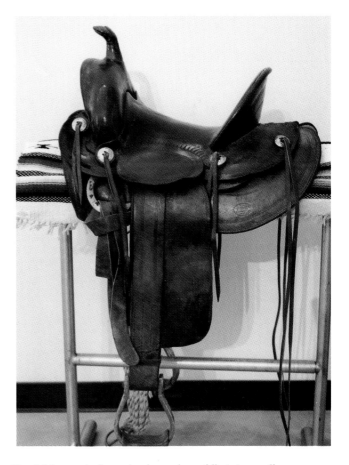

Frank Meanea is the maker here, the saddle is in excellent condition, a classic "deep seater," Frank Meanea, Cheyenne, Wyoming, 1873-1928. When he died the shop was given to Tom Cobry who later closed it. *Courtesy Paul and Marlene Snider.* $750-1250

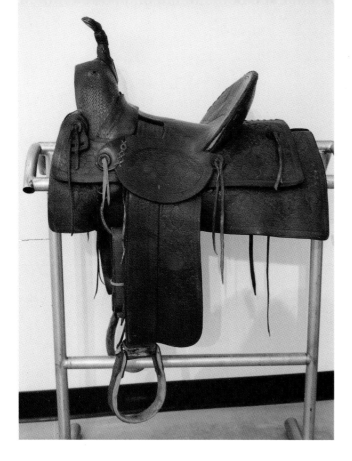

Hand made saddle with laced cantle, purported to have been used in World War I, c. 1900-1910. *Courtesy Paul and Marlene Snider.* $750-850

This saddle is marked "Miles City Saddlery, Miles City, Montana. Makers, Original Coggshall Saddles". It was owned by C.L. Sears, who was foreman for the Bar-M Ranch, Raft River, Idaho. 1913-1914. It is now owned by his grandson. *Courtesy C.L. Sears.* $1000-1200

Fred Allen Jennings was this saddle's original owner in 1912-1915. It is marked "Cable Rigged, Never Break, John Day, Oregon". The makers mark is obscured but is V.H. M.". *Courtesy of Alice Jennings Anderson.* $1200-1500

Makers mark on previous saddle.

George Lawrence saddle with novel full round metal oxbow stirrups, and poppy floral tooling, c. 1890s. *Private Collection.* $1700-2000

Fred Mueller saddle with unique built in tool holder, the saddle is in excellent condition and is quite rare, c. 1910-1930. It is a three quarter single rigged saddle. *Private Collection.*

Makers mark on previous saddle.

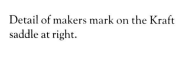

Detail of makers mark on the Kraft saddle at right.

Rare Kraft center fire with unmarked pockets, two and a half inch stirrup leathers, circle ring rawhide wrapped stirrups. Saddle is marked "A.A. Kraft Co. Spokane, Wt." c. late 1890s. *Private Collection.* $1500-2000

"A.A. Kraft" saddle three quarter single rigging, c. 1900, it has three inch stirrup leathers and Visalia stirrups. *Private Collection.* $1700-2200

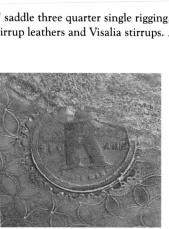

Detail makers mark on previous saddle.

Marked "Harpham Bros." on cartouche #101, it is a full double rigging with full tapaderos, c. 1914-1920. *Private Collection.* $1800-2200

Makers mark on cartouche.

Saddle is marked "R.T. Frazier, Pueblo, Co.", it is a full double rigging, with unique swivel stirrups, the cartouche with makers name is in seat and also on both fenders. It has attached staple-tool pouch on right side, c. 1910. *Private Collection.* $1700-2000

Detail of pouch on right side of previous saddle.

Detail of cartouche on previous saddle.

R.T. Frazier saddles were well marked.

Very rare "Sentinel Butte" from Sentinel Butte, North Dakota. This saddle represents one of two that was ever built, the other one is at the museum in Cody, Wyoming, c. 1900. *Private Collection.* $1800-2000

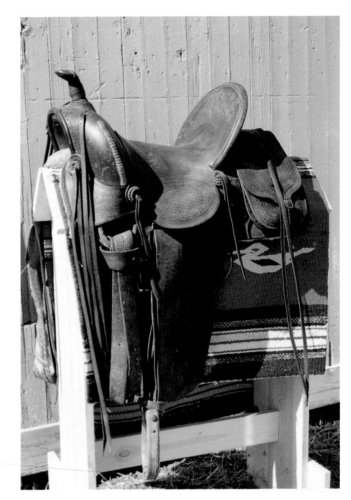

Marked "Los Angeles Saddlery and Finding Co." this saddle has original horse hair cinch. It has tooling design inside stirrups on the tread, c. 1905. *Private Collection.* $1700-2200

Al Furstnow, Miles City, Montana, used on a ranch in Western North Dakota…it has full tapaderos, and is a full single rigging, c. 1913-1914. *Private Collection.* $1700-2000

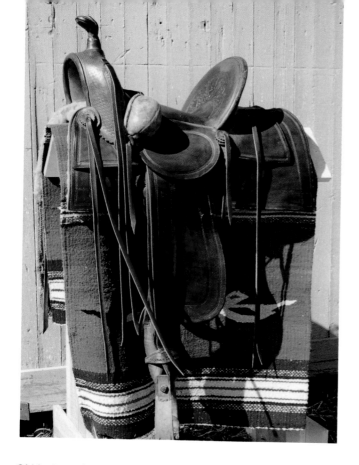

Detail of compass pocket on back of U.S. packer saddle. *Courtesy Paul and Marlene Snider.*

Old high cantle, border design, with double rigging and bucking rolls. It is in excellent condition, c. 1900s. *Private Collection.* $1800-2200

Old U.S. packer saddle in pristine condition with a compass pocket on back of cantle. *Courtesy Paul and Marlene Snider.* $1500-2000

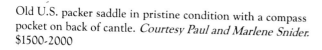

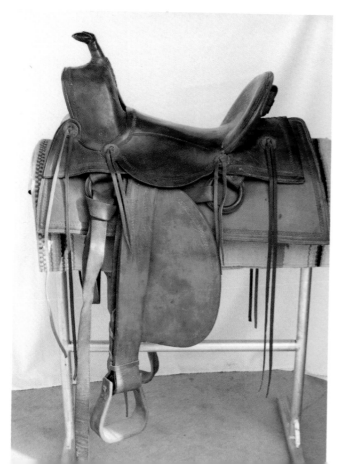

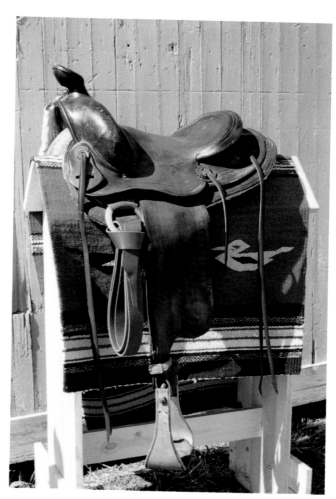

F.A. Meanea, saddle #8, 1936, it has a Bob Crosby roper tree in it. *Private Collection.* $1200-1500

Marked "N. Porter Co. Phoenix, Arizona" c. 1930s, this saddle is a newer version of a previous saddle company. It has a flat plate seven eighth rigging in it. *Private Collection.* $1700-2000

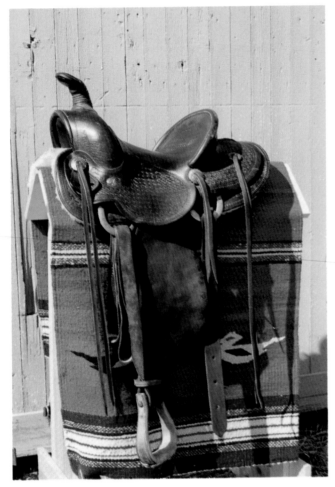

Marked "N. Porter Co. Phoenix, Arizona" with full double rigging, c. 1920s. *Private Collection.* $900-1200

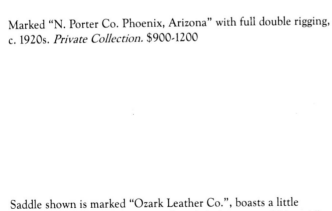

Saddle shown is marked "Ozark Leather Co.", boasts a little wonder tree, and is decorated with nickel silver spots. This saddle company worked out of Waco, Texas, and were the manufacturers of the "Saddle King" saddles. It has a full double rigging in it. *Private Collection.* $500-700

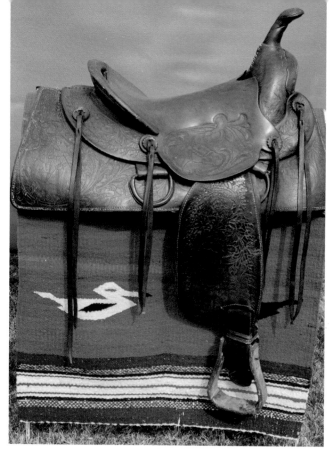

Detail of ornate carving on Hamley saddle.

Very rare and unique Hamley Trick Riders saddle, with cut out hand hold in cantle. Hand carved with ornate designs, it is a full double rigged saddle c. 1905-1910. *Courtesy William Scott Deatherage.* $2800-3000

Detail of cutout on cantle, Hamley and Co. made for Trick Rider. Hamley and Co. Saddle Makers have operated in Pendleton, Oregon, since 1905 until present time.

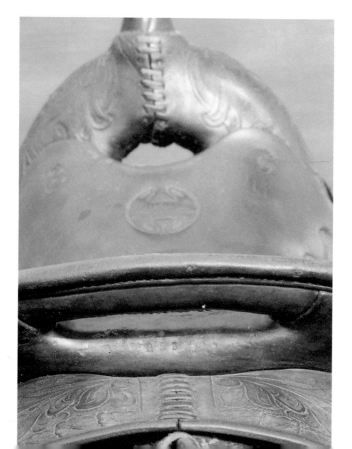

Interesting carving on Hamley saddle shown previously, depicting a man on horse with a quirt in his left hand.

21

Old hand made "bear trap" saddle, c. 1910, the left swell has been patched by the owner. *Courtesy Marlin Pool.* $300-400

Cartouche on saddle reads: "Hamley and Co. Circle H, Pendleton, Or.". This was Hamley's finest built saddle. With a gold medallion under the forks, it was called the "Gold Seal Edition", c. 1940. *Courtesy Roy and Jeanenne Williams.* $2500-3000

Hamley and Co. "Gold Edition" with brass medallion located under forks, c. 1940s. *Courtesy Don Rock.* $2500

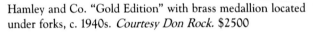

Youth saddle built by "Buck Steiner, Austin, Texas" with a small nine and half inch seat in it, c. 1930. *Courtesy Roy and Jeanenne Williams.* $1000-1500

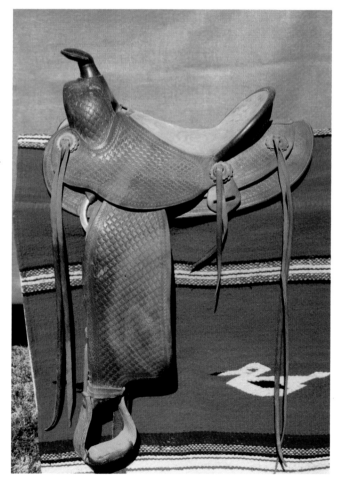

Hamley Special with bucking rolls. It has a cartouche naming the maker, c. 1930s. *Courtesy Don Rock.* $1500

J.C. Higgens hand carved saddle with fourteen inch seat, in nice condition, c. 1933. *Overton Collection.* $300-500

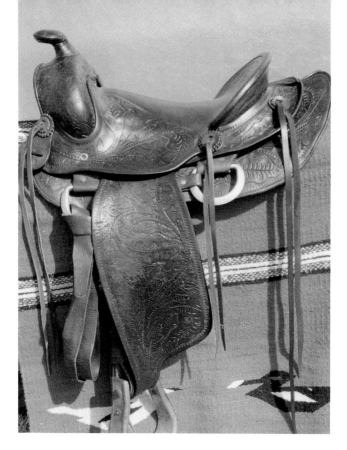

Miller and Stockman are the makers of this saddle with a fifteen inch seat in it, all hand made and hand carved. *Overton Collection.* $500-700

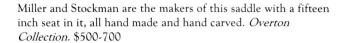

Colorado Saddlery is the maker of this saddle, which has a fifteen inch seat in it and is in good condition. *Overton Collection.* $500-700

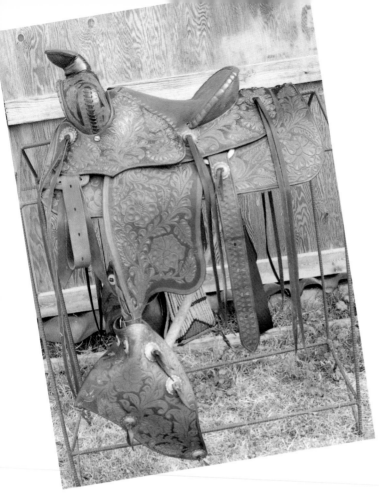

Name plate installed on back of trophy saddle.

Trophy saddle awarded to William Overton for All Around in 1948, made by Wilkerson Saddlery, Redmond, Oregon. It has full tapaderos, but also came with regular stirrups. *Overton Collection.* $1700-2000

Detail of wild rose conchos found on trophy saddle.

German silver studded parade saddle it is unmarked but attributed to Ted Flowers, Indiana, c. 1940s. *Courtesy Paul and Marlene Snider.* $1750-2200

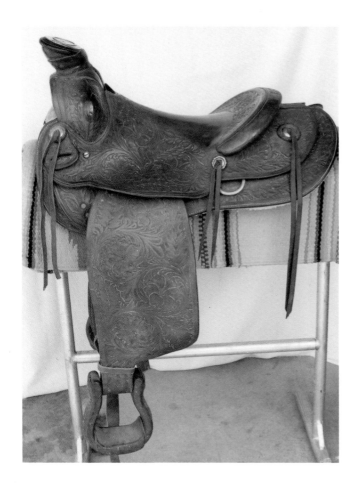

Saddle is a Visalia, marked "D.E. Walker Maker". It is c. 1940s and marked with number 24. *Courtesy Paul and Marlene Snider.* $1500-1700

Detail of horn cap on previous saddle, it is sterling silver and depicts a cowboy on a bucking horse.

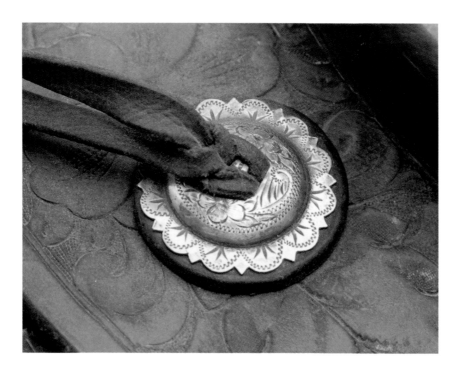

Detail of fancy conchos on the Visalia saddle, they are sterling silver tie conchos.

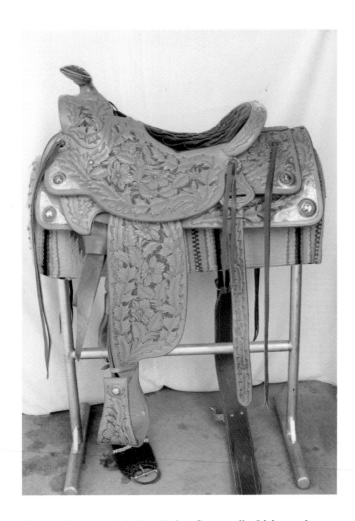

Cartouche of the Ray Holes saddle. Mr. Holes was a very talented saddlemaker, and proud of his work.

This saddle was built by Ray Holes, Grangeville, Idaho, and certainly illustrates how far the art of saddle making has been brought. *Courtesy Paul and Marlene Snider.* $6000-6500

Detail of sterling silver horn cap on the Ray Holes saddle.

Corner plates on skirts of the Ray Holes saddle.

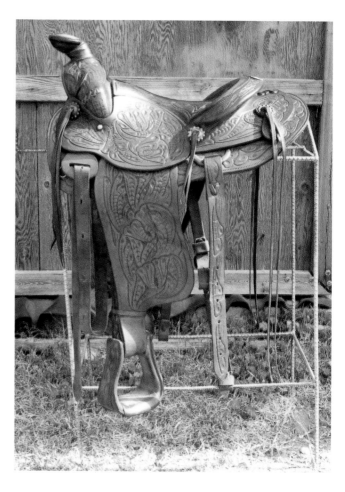

Saddle was built by the Late, Great, Charlie Baker from Baker, Oregon. It has matching saddle bags, sterling silver trim, and full leather covered stirrups, and has to be considered one of the finest saddles ever built in this century. *Overton Collection.* $5000-6000

A saddle built in the prison at McCallister, Oklahoma. It has beautiful carving, sterling silver trim, full leather covered stirrups, and is my own. *Overton Collection.* $1200-1700

Detail of leather carving and silver concho on the Charlie Baker saddle.

Silver tie concho on prison made saddle, showing detail of carving on leather.

CHAPTER TWO
SADDLE BAGS AND ACCESSORIES

SADDLE BAGS

Just as our modern day living and travelling incorporates the use of suitcases, briefcases, backpacks, and various other bags for the sake of convenience, so also did the cowboy life.

One of the best saddle accessories he could have was a good pair of saddle bags. Some of the items carried in them might have been a clean shirt, dry socks, extra neckerchief, tobacco, shaving gear, spare cartridges, and perhaps some playing cards or harmonica.

The life of the working cowboy on the range was sometimes a lonely one, and what he carried with him was often times the only pleasure or diversion he might have for weeks on end.

U.S. Cavalry issue saddle bags were not only used by the Cavalry, but by cowboys and drifters as well. The U.S. Cavalry bags were highly sought after by the cowboy for several reasons; they were larger and more serviceable and they had a canvas liner in them that could be removed and cleaned. They were also soft leather with large, double, or triple buckled closures. The model 1904 issue saddle bags seem to have been the most prolific and widely used.

The rare Doctor saddle bags are interesting in that they have a depth and dimension that the others do not, and therefore held more. They were often times made to specific orders by the Frontier Doctors, and were built with compartments for medicines, etc. They were almost always dyed black by the saddlemakers.

In 1880, a pair of plain leather saddle bags made by F.A. Meanea, Cheyenne, Wyoming, for example, would have cost the cowboy $3.50, and perhaps as high as $12 for the hand carved and fancy ones. Those same saddle bags today, in excellent condition, have brought as much as $600 to $900 at large cowboy Auctions.

U.S. Cavalry original government issue saddle bags with brass buckles and canvas lining, complete with spare reins and salt bag inside bags. *Courtesy Paul and Marlene Snider.* $600-700

Generally sought after are the ones with a built-in gun holster either on the inside or outside of the bag. Those particular ones seem to bring the high dollar amount, along with other distinct and unique type saddle bags.

There were basically three types of saddle bags made; the first being the large saddle bags that fit behind the cantle of the saddle and hung down on either side of the horse's rear end. They have a connecting leather piece that is cut with a contour so they fit nicely behind the saddle cantle. The second type includes the pommel bags, or bag, and these are designed with a large hole in either the connecting leather piece, or the single bag's strap, so that they can be hung over the horn of the saddle. Not quite as popular as the rear saddle bags, they were, however, handy for the cowboy to get into while still mounted.

The third variety of saddle bags are Saddle Pockets, which were generally smaller and deeper than the two previous types, and were sometimes termed "Saddle Cantenas." They were also designed as a one pocket bag with a small hole at the leather strap top, so they could be simply tied onto the saddle with a saddle string.

Another saddle accessory that played a big part in a cowboy's working day and life was the fence stapler puller bag. It was important in that it contained a very vital tool, the fence pliers. They were designed to enable the "fence rider" to either pull an old staple out of a fence post, or perhaps pound a new one in. Many cowboys took pride in the appearance of these small fence pliers bags the same as they did with the larger saddle bags.

All leather saddle bags should have the same kind of care for good preservation that saddles are given.

These saddle bags are marked "Crozier Saddlery" Lewiston, Idaho. *Courtesy Paul and Marlene Snider.* $200-300

This pair of saddle bags is marked "Dale Pack Station" made by Gordie Dale in Yakima, Washington. *Courtesy Paul and Marlene Snider.* $300-400

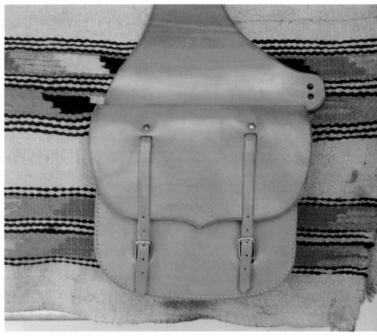

The Late, Great Charlie Baker is the maker of these bags, made in a similar design as the U.S. Cavalry bags. *Courtesy Paul and Marlene Snider.* $400-500

Hand carved leather saddle bags, maker unknown. *Courtesy Paul and Marlene Snider.* $300-400

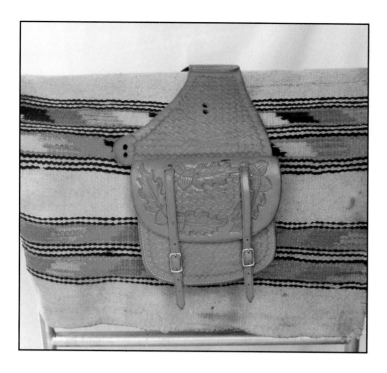

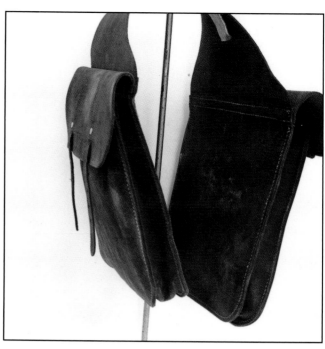

Another pair by the Great Charlie Baker, from Baker, Oregon…a finer saddlemaker never lived! Carved with unique acorns and basket weave, the bags are one of a kind. *Courtesy Paul and Marlene Snider.* $500-600

Rough out leather, the saddle bags shown are home made. *Courtesy Marlin Pool.* $75-100

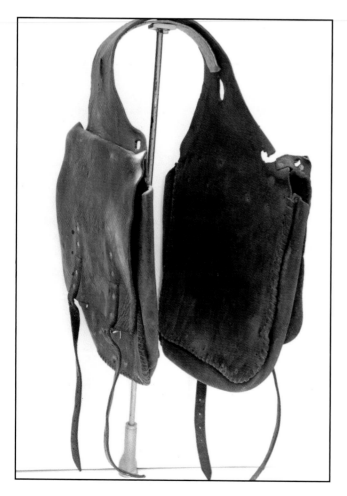

Saddle bags made of smooth leather that has been home tanned, showing some wear, c. 1928. *Courtesy Marlin Pool.* $75-100

These saddle bags are all hand carved and were made in prison. *Courtesy Larry and Aileen Fisher.* $250-350

Extra large smooth leather bags, c. 1930. The saddlemaker did not mark them. *Courtesy Larry and Aileen Fisher.* $300-400

Large hand tooled saddle bags in excellent condition. *Courtesy Larry and Aileen Fisher.* $275-375

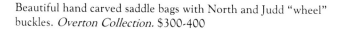

Bags are marked "The Western Saddle Mfg. Co." Denver, Colorado. *Courtesy Larry and Aileen Fisher.* $375-475

Beautiful hand carved saddle bags with North and Judd "wheel" buckles. *Overton Collection.* $300-400

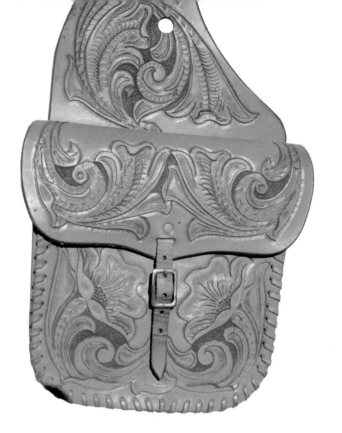

Belt type pockets were also made by saddlemakers and were sometimes used with other saddle bags. *Courtesy Larry and Aileen Fisher.* $150-175

Hand carved saddle bags laced together with leather lacing. *Overton Collection.* $200-300

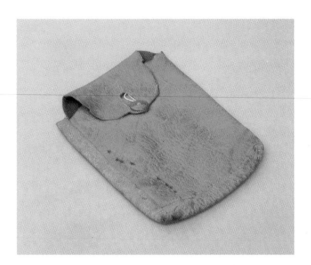

Soft leather belt pocket, probably hand made. *Courtesy Larry and Aileen Fisher.* $50-125

U.S. Cavalry issue saddle pockets, attributed to time of conflict with Pancho Villa, and most likely held guns. They are in excellent condition. *Overton Collection.* $300-400

Unmarked saddle bags either pommel or cantle, they are smooth leather with border design and a full flap, c. 1890s. *Private Collection.* $300-500

Unique "Mountain Man" backpack, hand made entirely of elk hide and lined with canvas. *Courtesy Paul and Marlene Snider.* $500-600

Attributed to "Conley Bros., Billings, Montana", the saddle bags are basket weave stamped, c. 1940. They have been well used. *Courtesy Roy and Jeanenne Williams.* $300-500

Saddle pockets are marked "F.A. Meanea, Cheyenne, Wyoming", c. 1910. *Private Collection.* $750-1000

Bear skin, hair side out pommel bags with an inside holster for pistol. The leather is floral carved, c. 1890s. *Private Collection.* $600-800

Inside view of previous bear skin pommel bags.

Saddle bags are marked "Denver Mfg. Co. Denver, Col." They are smooth leather with a border design, c. late 1890s. *Private Collection.* $500-700

Small saddle bags with inside knife and fence tool scabbard, unmarked, c. 1910. *Private Collection.* $700-900

Hand tooled saddle bags with two extra pockets on inside. *Private Collection.* $700-900

Hand tooled and carved saddle bags in excellent condition. *Private Collection.* $500-700

Plain leather with a border design, these saddle bags have seen some use, c. 1890s. *Private Collection.* $200-300

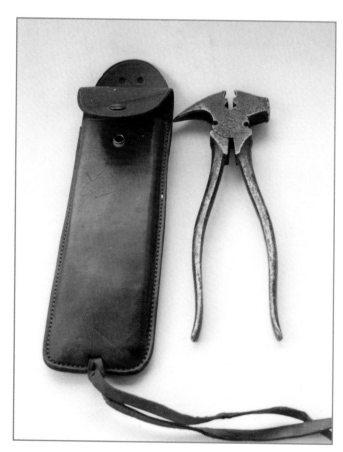

Fence tool scabbard, often kept tied to the saddle. *Overton Collection.* $50-75

Hand tooled scabbard for fence tool with a North and Judd "cartwheel" buckle. *Overton Collection.* $100-125

TAPADEROS

We can thank the Spanish for tapaderos, or "taps" as they are often called. Taps go back as far as 1830, and have many different styles. They are most always named for their overall appearance, i.e.: "monkey nose," "hog snout," "eagle billed," and so on.

The taps served more than one useful purpose; they kept the boot from slipping straight through the stirrup and also kept the foot and boot safe in heavy thorn and brush country. They are actually just a leather "hood" for the stirrup, and are sometimes referred to as "toe fenders."

Tapaderos eventually evolved into fancy tooled varieties that added greatly to the appearance and sometimes even the balance of the saddle. The saddles that are equipped with a fancy pair of tapaderos in recent years have become very desirable for dress parades and shows in the West. Some cowboys have taps and a pair of regular leather covered stirrups for one saddle, thereby making an interchange possible, depending on the particular use anticipated for the saddle at the time. Leather covered stirrups were generally available at saddle shops through out the West and were quite often sold separately from the saddle, either as replacements or additions to the saddle the cowboy already owned.

Hand tooled pair of saddle tapaderos. They are the "eagle bill" design and shape. *Overton Collection.* $250-350

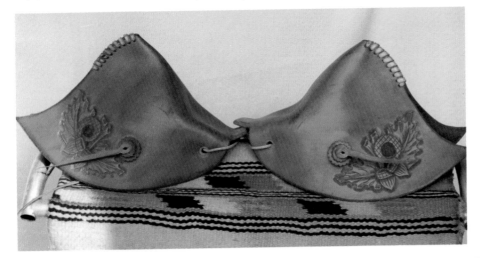

Hand tooled saddle tapaderos made by the very talented Late Charlie Baker, who is missed greatly by the Western cowboy World. *Courtesy Paul and Marlene Snider.* $350-450

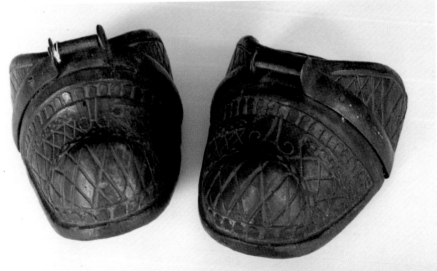

Fancy carved wood, enclosed toe, Mexican saddle stirrups, they are very old. *Courtesy Paul and Marlene Snider.* $500-600

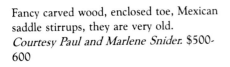

Early Mexican, Leonardo Cardenas wooden stirrups, with carved toes. They came out of California in the 1870s. *Courtesy Paul and Marlene Snider.* $600-700

Oxbow stirrups, hand stretched and covered with rawhide and leather. *Courtesy Roy and Jeanenne Williams.* $65-75

Rawhide stirrups hand covered and side seamed with inside sewn stitching, all stitches are invisible on outside. They are very durable and long lasting. Handmade by Roy Williams. *Courtesy Roy and Jeanenne Williams.* $80-100

Hand braided rawhide quirt. *Courtesy Roy and Jeanenne Williams.* $400-500

Hand braided rawhide hobbles. Quite often cowboys would carry a pair of these, and when letting his horse rest and graze a while, he attached them to horse's ankles so the horse would remain in a small area. *Courtesy Paul and Marlene Snider.* $350-450

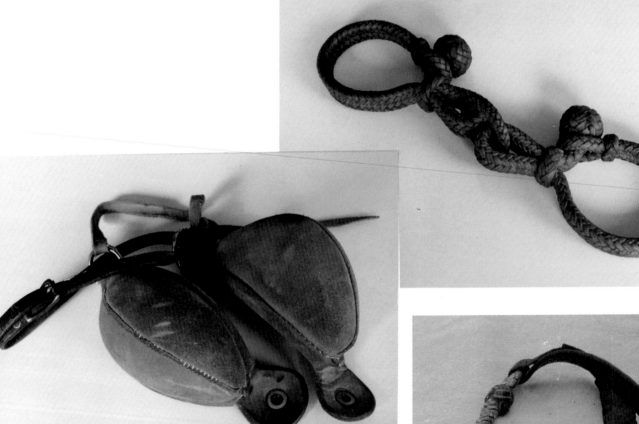

Pair of rough out bucking rolls, which attach to saddle for protection. *Courtesy Paul and Marlene Snider.* $150-200

Rawhide braided quirt, hand braided by the late Dave Stirewalt, a genuine cowboy all of his life. *Courtesy Bob and Judy Bertsch.* $175-225

CHAPTER THREE

BRIDLES AND REINS

BRIDLES

While it is true that a cowboy's saddle has always been his primary piece of equipment, his bridle would have to fall into line as second. A good bridle had to meet certain necessary standards for the man using it. For example, for safety's sake, it had to be durable and it had to be easy to put on a horse in very little time. It had to be fairly adjustable as to size of head stall, and with a practical bit in it.

The most popular bridle was generally a split ear head stall with braided or leather reins and a curb bit. This was the combination that offered the most ease of use.

Bridles take form in many various materials: leather, rawhide, rope, horse hair, and twine. If a man got into trouble and needed a make shift bridle in a hurry, he has been known to even make one from his own belt and a few quick cuts from a sharp knife!

The simplest bridle ever devised was the Indian War bridle. It was fashioned from one long piece of leather or rawhide, cut into a strap. It was then looped around the horse's lower jaw at the middle of the strap, and the two long ends brought up to the mounted man for reins. Nothing could have been simpler to make or use. Surprisingly, it gave good control.

A standard bridle is actually comprised of three basic parts or components: bit, head stall, and reins. Variations and combinations of these three components are almost endless.

The three basic head stalls for a bridle are:

#1: California brow band style. It has a brow band, nose band, and throat latch.

#2: Split ear style. Sometimes one ear is all that is split, sometimes two loops are made, or split. This head stall is held in place on the horse by putting either one or both ears of the horse through the split.

Old hand tooled head stall with California brow band, it carries four tie conchos and a Crockett spade bit, c. 1940. *Courtesy Marlin Pool.* $200-225

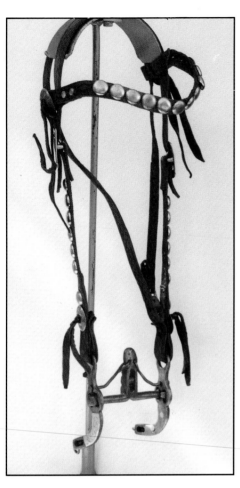

Nickel silver spots adorn this early California brow band style head stall, c. 1920s. It has a short shanked, shop made bit in it. *Courtesy Marlin Pool.* $200-250

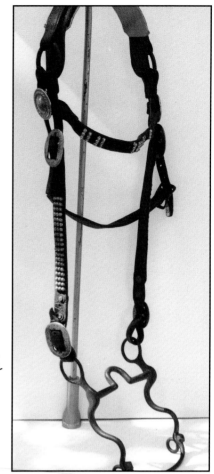

California brow band style with rather unusual nickel studs, has an "S" shank North and Judd bit in it that is a medium port, c. 1915. *Courtesy Marlin Pool.* $300-325

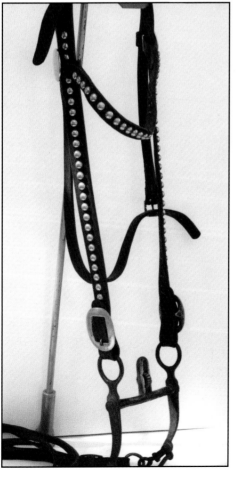

The head stall has North and Judd buckles on it, and is bearing nickel silver spots, c. 1923. It has an old iron Buermann half breed bit in it. *Courtesy Marlin Pool.* $250-275

North and Judd "war time" buckles on head stall, August Buermann "bird" bit, missing its slobber chains. The spots on this one are brass, c. 1914-1918. *Courtesy Marlin Pool.* $300-350

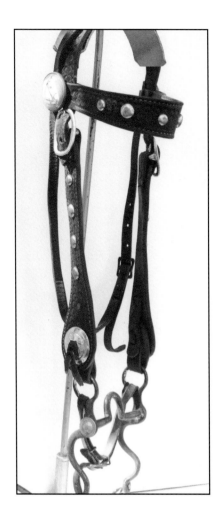

North and Judd "Texas" bit, California brow band style head stall, carrying two lovely old "horse head" rosettes and nickel silver spots, c. 1910. *Courtesy Marlin Pool.* $350-400

Sterling silver conchos decorate the head stall and rawhide braided knots on leather braided reins. The half breed bit is Visalia. Brow band is decorated with three silver conchos. *Overton Collection.* $900-1200

Rosettes are always a big plus to some of the older head stalls and bridles. This one was found on an old 1930s head stall with nickel silver spots surrounding it. *Courtesy Marlin Pool.* $350-375

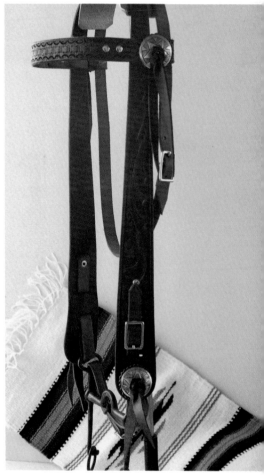

California brow band style with two German silver conchos and a plain port bit in it, c. 1930s. *Overton Collection.* $300-350

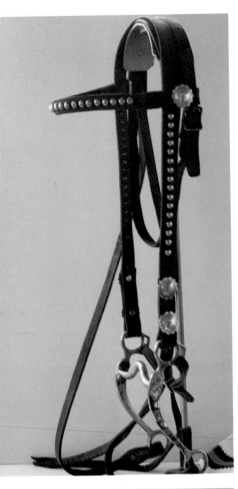

Early California style with sterling silver conchos and nickel silver spots on head stall. It has silver overlays on the port bit, c. 1930s. *Overton Collection.* $750-900

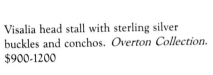

Visalia head stall with sterling silver buckles and conchos. *Overton Collection.* $900-1200

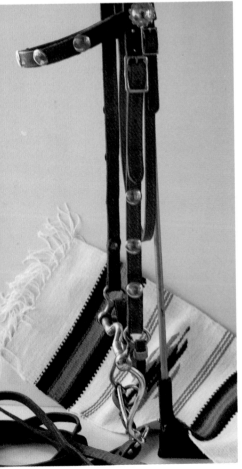

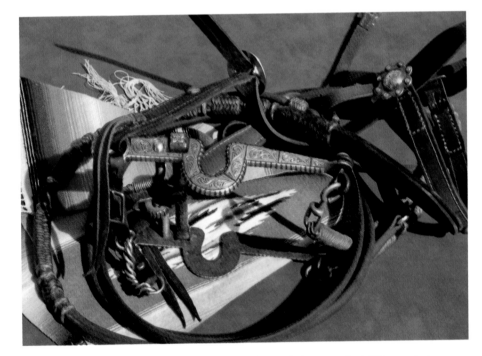

California brow band style head stall with a bit marked: "USA Steel, McKinnon" it has a sterling silver concho on bit and several on head stall. *Overton Collection.* $700-900

The spade bit is marked "Fleming", the head stall is a California style with brow band, and rawhide braided reins complete this working cowboy's outfit, c. 1940. *Courtesy Roy and Jeanenne Williams.* $1300-1500

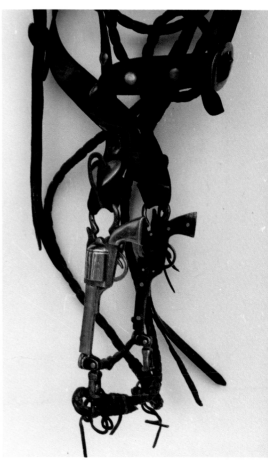

Bit is marked "A. Tietjen" and is a Mona Lisa half breed with loose jaws and Colorado style cheek plates. The head stall is a Circle Y with silver mounted brow band and silver conchos and buckles. *Courtesy Roy and Jeanenne Williams.* $750-1250

California brow band style, this particular bridle and bit is an exceptional example of just how fancy some became. The bit is inscribed with "W.F. Cody", it was found in an old barn on the Wyoming border in 1937. *Courtesy Paul and Marlene Snider.* (Too valuable to estimate)

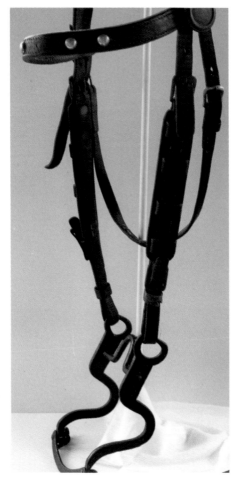

Original bit and head stall it is Military issue during the Civil War, bit has mark "CSA" Confederate States America. They were used later by cowboys, but it is unusual and rare to find them in as good of condition as this one is. *Courtesy William Scott Deatherage.* $800-1200

Detail of mark inside the Civil War port bit.

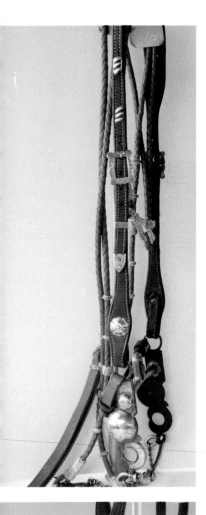

Bit is a half breed attributed to Mike Morales, it has lead filled silver conchos. The head stall is a split ear style, with silver buckles and ornamentation. *Overton Collection.* $1000-1500

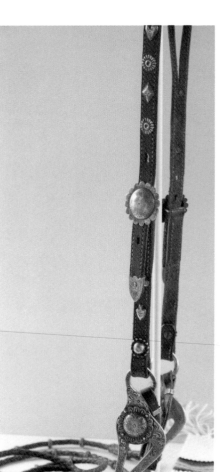

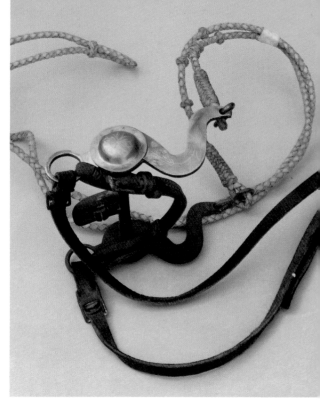

Bit is Walla Walla Prison made half breed with German silver overlay, leather head stall, and rawhide reins. *Courtesy Larry and Aileen Fisher.* $350-550

Santa Barbara spade with a split ear head stall and hand braided reins. It is a beautiful bridle. *Courtesy Paul and Marlene Snider.* $1000-1200

Double split ear head stall, with Fleming half breed bit. Silver "Card Suit" decoration on head stall, and large sterling silver concho. Braided reins complete the bridle. *Overton Collection.* $1500-2200

Double split ear head stall with throat latch and sterling silver overlay on the port bit. The conchos on the head stall are sterling silver with gold horse heads in center. Braided reins with rawhide braided knots and ferrules make this a very nice bridle. *Overton Collection.* $1200-1700

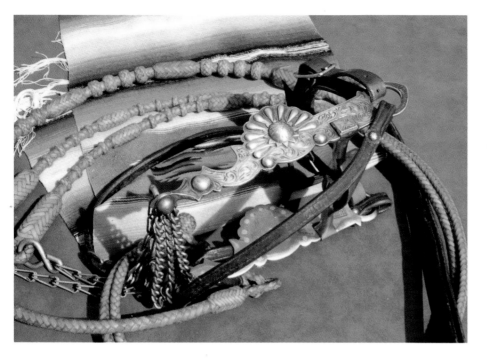

This bit is marked "Fleming", it is a
Salinas mouth piece, loose jaw, with lovely
sterling silver engraved cheek plates. It
has rawhide braided reins, and is marked
on the romal "Ashs's Rawhide Leather,
Kooskia, Id." *Courtesy Roy and Jeanenne
Williams.* $1500-2000

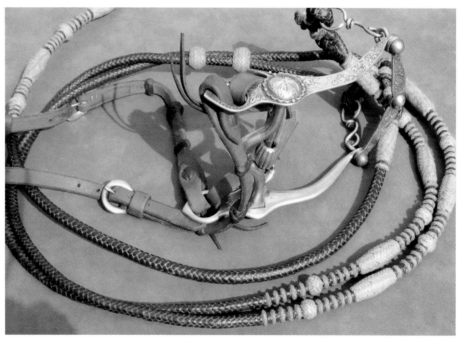

Garcia half breed bit, with very rare and
unique rawhide braided reins, the dark
part on reins is kangaroo, and has rawhide
braided "buttons" and oak leaves carved
on the romal. *Courtesy Roy and Jeanenne
Williams.* $1500-2500

This port bit was hand made by Roy
Williams. It has silver overlays with tiny
"fleur de lis" stamped in each silver bar
with plain leather head stall and reins.
Courtesy Roy and Jeanenne Williams.
$750-850

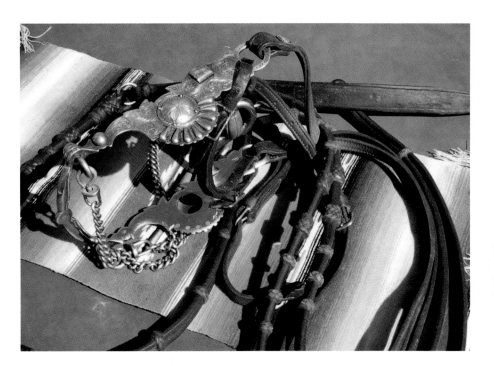

Bit is marked "Vogt", it has a Mona Lisa mouth piece, with beautiful silver cheek plates. Rawhide braided knots decorate the reins. *Courtesy Roy and Jeanenne Williams.* $900-1200

Texas Star bit is marked with "A. Tietjen" "Reno, Nv." and the reins are rawhide braided with rawhide braided knots on the head stall. *Courtesy Roy and Jeanenne Williams.* $1000-1500

Bit is a silver mounted half breed made by Roy Williams patterned after a ring bit with similar design cheek plates. Rawhide braided reins and split ear head stall, plain leather. *Courtesy Roy and Jeanenne Williams.* $1000-1200

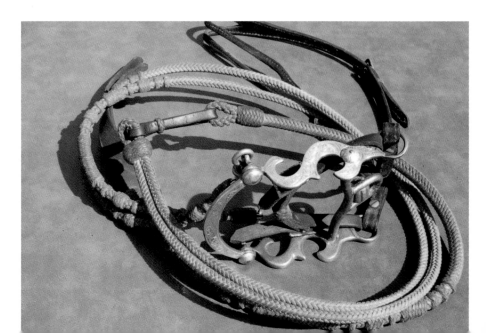

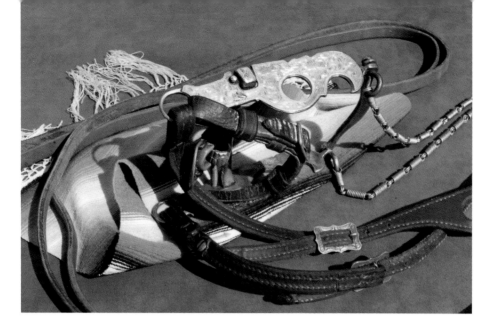

Marked "E.M." on the bit, this is a low spade with Santa Barbara cheek plates. Visalia silver buckles on head stall. *Courtesy Roy and Jeanenne Williams.* $800-900

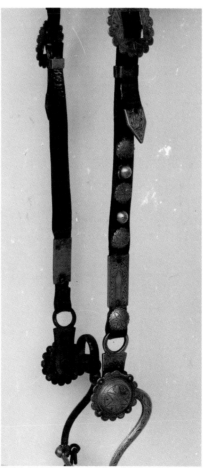

Argentine bit is marked "Cabbilero", and the bit is silver with gold spots. *Courtesy Paul and Marlene Snider.* $1200-1500

Old Garcia bit in a fancy head stall with sterling silver conchos and buckles. The head stall is split ear style. *Courtesy Paul and Marlene Snider.* $900-1200

Silver mounted bit with split ear head stall and silver conchos, sporting a pair of exceptional braided reins. *Courtesy Paul and Marlene Snider.* $900-1200

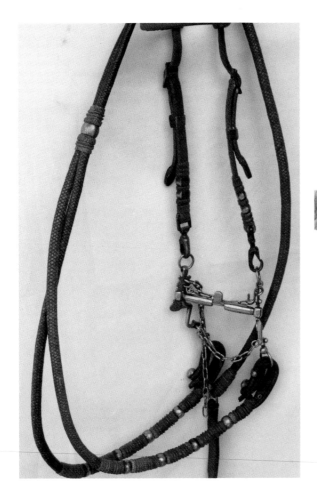

Detail of reins on Argentine snaffle-bridle.

Argentine snaffle and fancy bridle with very fine braided leather reins and head stall. They are interspersed with silver ferrules. *Courtesy Paul and Marlene Snider.* $600-800

Deer Lodge, Montana, horse hair braided bridle. It is ornamented with horse hair tassels. *Courtesy Paul and Marlene Snider.* $3000-4000

Horse hair bridle braided by Native Americans, featuring rosettes with roses in them. *Overton Collection.* $900-1200

#3: Hackamore style. The hackamore style is fitted with a bosal, or in simple terms, a braided loop for around the nose of the horse, generally fashioned of braided rawhide, it is made with a Turk's Knot for under the jaw of the horse. When the reins are pulled up, the knot presses on the under jaw where nerves are, and the horse is thus controlled. This method of reining is as efficient as the bridle with a solid bit in it. The hackamore is always found with a braided or twisted horse hair mecate or a braided rope mecate, and is never used with leather reins. The mecate being the actual reins in this case that are attached to the bosal.

Today the overall value of a good bridle is most often determined by the bit that is found in it, and the amount of silver ornamentation that it bears. Often times the makers mark, if it has one, also plays a part in determining value. Without a doubt the most desirable, collectible, and expensive of these are the horse hair braided bridles. They are very rare and difficult to find at any price. Some of these have been braided by Indians, and some by inmates at prisons down through the years. If they are in any kind of preservation or condition at all, they always bring high dollar.

There are a few "Horse Hair Workers" today who are doing excellent work, so one needs to be cautious in determining if it is old "hair work" or contemporary. The fact that it is new should in no way diminish value, for it is a true work of art no matter when it may have been made, but there are collectors who prefer the older work. The very best care you can give a braided horse hair bridle is to store it well with moth balls. Moths will prefer the natural un-dyed hair, so they are particularly susceptible.

Silver mounted bridles with a good silver mounted bit in it have also been known to bring very high dollar amounts at present day cowboy auctions. They sometimes carry the most ornate kind of silver conchos and

ornamentation. Card suits are a popular silver ornamentation, and small floral designs are also popular. They dress up a head stall made of leather very nicely. Another popular ornamentation from out of the past is the rosettes, sometimes still to be found on head stalls that are very old. They were made of metal backing with a glass dome over some item such as a rose or a bucking cowboy. They are very desirable rare, and costly when they are found.

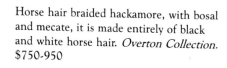

Horse hair braided hackamore, with bosal and mecate, it is made entirely of black and white horse hair. *Overton Collection.* $750-950

Argentine hackamore with silver ferrules and a fancy medallion. *Courtesy Paul and Marlene Snider.* $600-700

Bosal is hand braided by Duff Severe, Pendleton, Oregon, the "Turks Knot" has a "Texas Star" braided into it at the bottom. The mecate is horse hair, three quarter inches around. *Courtesy Roy and Jeanenne Williams.* $300-400

Detail of "Turks Knot" with "Texas Star".

Ranch made bosal with horse hair mecate, the head stall is done in leather that is Spanish lacing. *Courtesy Roy and Jeanenne Williams.* $150-200

Rawhide braided bosal with large fancy rawhide braided "Turks Knot". *Courtesy Roy and Jeanenne Williams.* $200-250

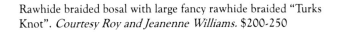

Latigo leather hand braided bosal with horse hair mecate. It is unusual to see bosals done in latigo instead of braided rawhide. *Courtesy Roy and Jeanenne Williams.* $200-250

Slender rawhide braided bosal with small "Turks Knot". *Overton Collection.* $50-75

Old hand braided rawhide bosal with a tasseled "Turks Knot" which has seen a lot of use. *Overton Collection.* $25-45

REINS

Bridle reins take two basic forms: flat leather and round braided leather. Generally they are two separate lines, with the exception of roping reins. A roping rein is a one line loop of a rein, which when dropped (in order for the cowboy to throw his lariat on a cow) they stay up around the horse's neck within reach to the cowboy, once the loop is thrown. Split reins would, of course, be dropped and lost to the ground. A roping rein, naturally, has no romal, the romal being the tapered leather two piece "popper" at the end of the rein.

In modern day collector circles, reins are like any other collectible, the more elaborate they are the more collectible they become. Of course, a plain flat leather rein would have taken much less time to make than an intricately braided rawhide rein with knots and ferrules. The most beautiful reins are the hand braided rawhide reins with sterling silver ferrules, and small knots. Naturally, they are the most sought after.

In an old 1902 Sears Roebuck Catalog, a fine "Mexican hand braided" bridle and reins sold for $6.95, but in today's cowboy Auctions a good pair of hand braided reins have brought as high as $1,800.

Hand braiding leather or rawhide reins is an art all in itself, and as in all particular arts, there are proven Masters. In this case, the work of Luis B. Ortega qualifies as such. Mr. Ortega sometimes marked his work, and in the case of braided reins, that mark is found in the romal. His work is highly desirable and collectible, and if you are ever fortunate enough to see and actually feel some of his work, you will quickly understand why. There is a tight finish to his braiding technique that none other seem to accomplish. The work is truly beautiful. Another Master Rawhider is Israel Medina, his work is quality *par excellence.*

Often times the tightness of the braid and the number of small knots incorporated into the rein is the deciding factor as to quality. Never wet or oil braided rawhide. The Latigo braided leather reins can be saddle soaped for softness and cleaning.

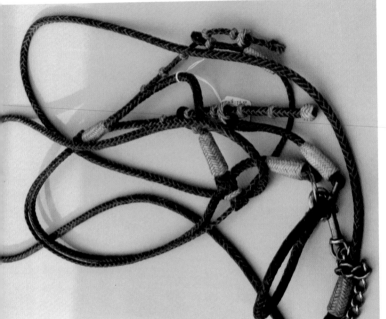

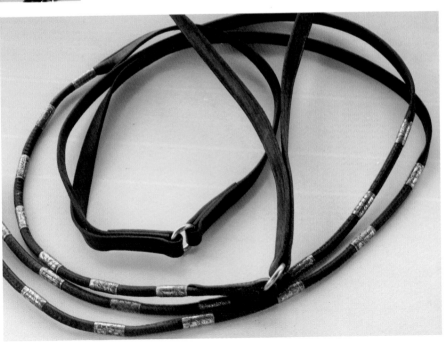

Hand braided reins with rawhide leather knots and ferrules. *Courtesy Larry and Aileen Fisher.* $150-175

Round leather braided reins with silver ferrules. *Overton Collection.* $200-300

Rawhide braided reins with leather romal. *Overton Collection.* $150-200

Braided latigo reins with rawhide knots and trim. *Overton Collection.* $150-200

Fancy hand braided leather reins with a very tight braid and exceptional design. The reins have over 100 knots. *Overton Collection.* $300-400

Braided latigo reins with rawhide knots.
Overton Collection. $150-200

Braided latigo reins with long romal.
Overton Collection. $50-75

Spanish braided leather reins made by
Robert Bertsch, Stanfield, Oregon.
Courtesy Bob and Judy Bertsch. $50-75

Pair of rawhide reins with a long leather
romal, it made a very durable set. *Overton
Collection.* $100-150

CHAPTER FOUR

RIATAS, BREAST COLLARS, MARTINGALES

"Un-Educated Leather"
"Yep, Rawhide sure come handy for the Western Pioneer
To git it, all he had to do was skin him out a steer
Of course its got one failin', for it stretches when its wet
But "tough as Rawhide" is a phrase the West cannot forget
They asked me, "What is Rawhide?"...its un-educated leather
But strong like them that used it, and it held the West together!"

S. Omar Barker

RIATAS

A riata is a hand braided lasso made of rawhide and usually braided to a forty or sixty foot of length. There are a few that have been twisted instead of braided, but that is an exception and not the rule.

Riatas were introduced by the Vaqueros as a part of cattle handling in the open spaces of early California. They are a rare and hard to find piece of cowboy equipment from the past, originally termed "La Reata" by the Spanish. Since the art of "rawhiding," as it is called, is being done less and less, even newly braided Riatas are difficult to find. Rawhiding in any form is rapidly becoming a lost art today.

Years ago the braided rawhide riata was all a Cowboy had for a lasso, but because they had weak spots, and would get slick in heavy rain, they were replaced with the stronger twisted grass ropes made from hemp or sisal and were readily accepted by the working cowboy as a better alternative to the braided riata.

Most of the modern day working cowboys that are left around the country are now using poly or plastic rope. Other than a very few rawhide braided riatas that are being made today, the only available rope for lassos on the market is made of poly or nylon.

A cowboy's Riata was the one piece of equipment that doubled as a working tool and also afforded him pleasure and enjoyment. One of the best pastimes he had was in some friendly "loop throwing" contests, and competitions among fellow trail hands on a lazy day off.

Today, hand braided Riatas are generally valued as to their length and condition. They are best kept dry, if possible, to preserve them. If they are dampened with water, they become slick, but return to original stiffness upon drying again. Contrary to leather items, rawhide never requires oiling or saddle soaping.

BREAST COLLARS, MARTINGALES

In order to distinguish a breast collar from a martingale, one only has to remember that a martingale circles the horse's neck, and a breast collar does not. Both are serious pieces of equipment for the working cowboy, especially if he is working in steep terrain.

The breast collar in this country most likely came into existence as an evolution, or one step up from pack saddle rigging. A good pack saddle secures both front and back on the animal, and must be especially well secured in order to carry the oftentimes huge loads on the saddle.

A breast collar fastens to the saddle in front across the chest of the horse and thereby holds the saddle in place, keeping it from slipping or sliding when horse and rider are on an uphill climb, or in the case of competition roping when a horse makes sudden lunges forward.

Neither martingales or breast collars were used by the old time cowboy or trail hands as a part of their daily equipment, unless they were working cattle in the high country. They are very time consuming to put on and take off. Old early saddles were not equipped with the rings to attach a breast collar to, but more contemporary saddles almost always are. Sometimes new saddles are built today with a matching breast collar and or a matching martingale, and thereby complement the overall appearance of the saddled horse.

The value of a breast collar or martingales is usually determined today by the amount of silver it carries, and of course, age and makers marks also play a part in evaluation.

Breast collars and martingales should be cared for in the same way as saddles are. They can be saddle soaped with a good liquid glycerin saddle soap on sheep wool in order to clean them safely, and then polished with a rubbing of good quality Neatsfoot Oil.

The breast collars that are lined with sheep wool should be stored with moth balls, and in a good place that is safe from mice. Nothing is more disappointing than pulling out of storage a nice old piece of cowboy equipment and find that either mice or moths have damaged it beyond repair.

Hand braided rawhide riata made by Louis Ortega, it is the desired length and a very tight braid. *Courtesy Paul and Marlene Snider.* $500-600

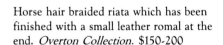
Horse hair braided riata which has been finished with a small leather romal at the end. *Overton Collection.* $150-200

Contemporary working lasso with rawhide covered hondo.
Overton Collection. $40-50

Wild cow halter which would have been used when a cow had to be roped, haltered, and led in for one reason or another. *Overton Collection.* $25-45

Bull rope, used in early rodeo rides. *Overton Collection.* $25-45

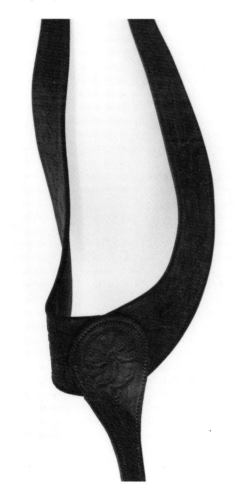

Leather tooled martingale, c. 1940s. *Courtesy Marlin Pool.* $50-75

Studded martingale, c. 1920s. *Courtesy Larry and Aileen Fisher.* $100-150

Popular heart shaped martingale with nickel silver spots, c. 1920s. *Courtesy Larry and Aileen Fisher.* $175-200

Heart studded martingale, c. 1930s. *Courtesy Larry and Aileen Fisher.* $50-75

Ornate nickel studded martingale with fancy rosette in center of heart. *Courtesy Bob and Judy Bertsch.* $300-400

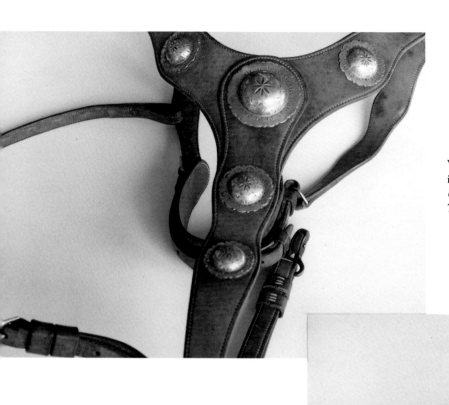

Visalia martingale with lovely old conchos in sterling silver, in excellent condition. *Courtesy Paul and Marlene Snider.* $600-750

Keyston is the maker of this martingale with sterling silver concho depicting a bucking horse. *Courtesy Paul and Marlene Snider.* $500-700

Detail of bucking horse on concho of Keyston martingale.

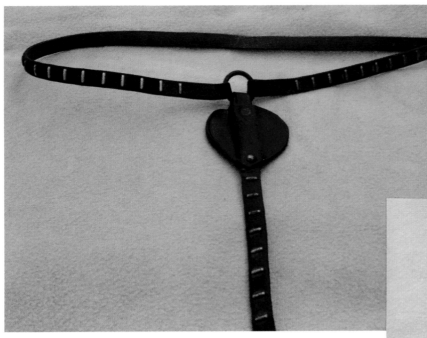

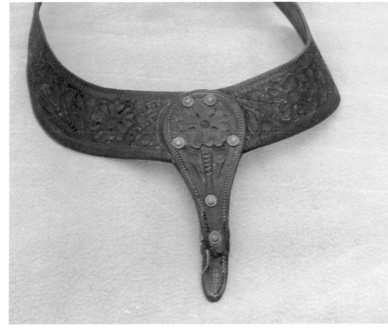

Running martingale made of saddle skirting leather. They were used to help keep the horse's head down, if he was prone to "throwing his head." *Courtesy Bob and Judy Bertsch.* $125-150

Martingale has long bar studs in nickel silver, c. 1910-1920. *Courtesy Bob and Judy Bertsch.* $125-150

Breast collar which says "Judy" on front and is hand tooled. Maker was Ray Olsen, Redmond, Oregon. *Courtesy Bob and Judy Bertsch.* $125-175

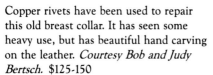

Copper rivets have been used to repair this old breast collar. It has seen some heavy use, but has beautiful hand carving on the leather. *Courtesy Bob and Judy Bertsch.* $125-150

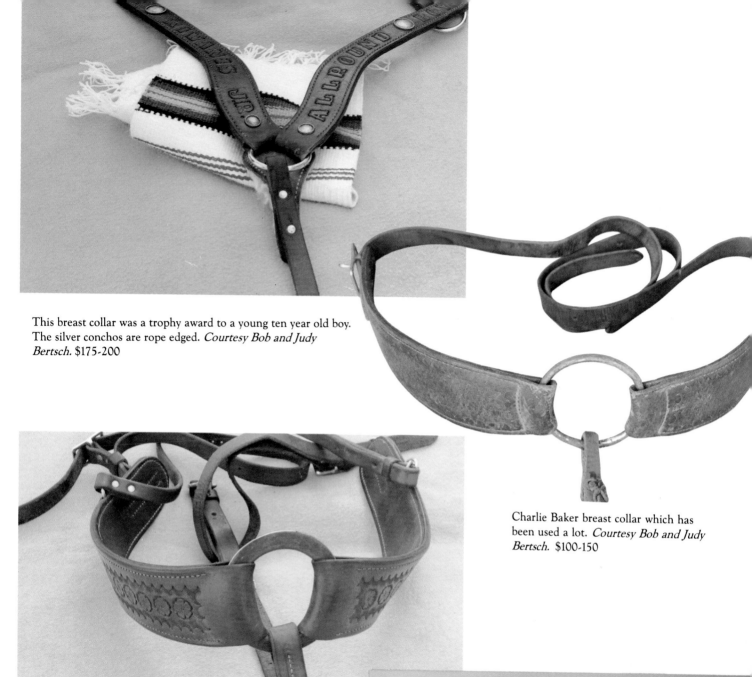

This breast collar was a trophy award to a young ten year old boy. The silver conchos are rope edged. *Courtesy Bob and Judy Bertsch.* $175-200

Charlie Baker breast collar which has been used a lot. *Courtesy Bob and Judy Bertsch.* $100-150

Hand tooled breast collar by Charlie Baker. (Yes folks, Charlie was a blessing to the cowboys of Oregon and the whole Northwest!) *Overton Collection.* $150-200

This breast collar is lined with sheepskin and is in excellent condition. It carries North and Judd buckles. *Overton Collection.* $200-250

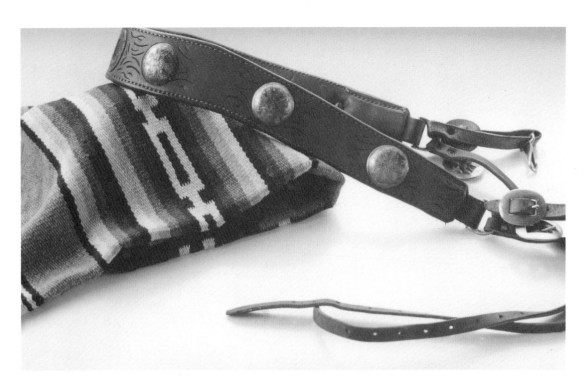

Six large domed, sterling silver conchos decorate this breast collar. *Overton Collection.* $350-450

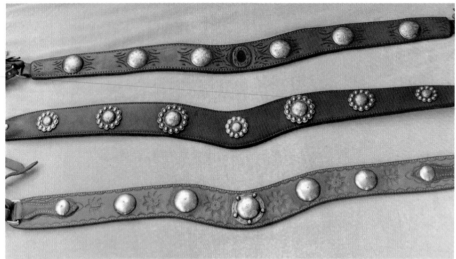

Grouping of three breast collars, all in working condition. *Overton Collection.* $300-800 each

Detail of concho on bottom breast collar.

This breast collar was completely hand made and sewn one stitch at a time, then decorated with Garcia conchos. *Overton Collection.* $600-800

Detail of Garcia concho.

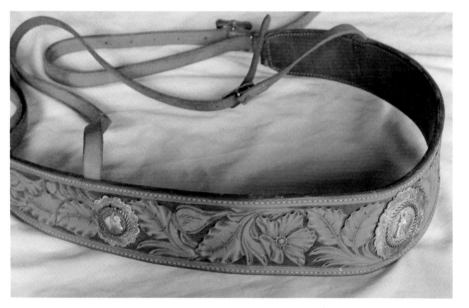

Ray Holes is the maker, it is finely carved and decorated with gold horse head conchos. *Courtesy Paul and Marlene Snider.* $750-900

Detail of gold horse heads on concho of the Ray Holes breast collar.

CHAPTER FIVE
CHAPS

The Vaquero called them his "chaparejos," the American cowboy shortened it to "chaps," pronounced "shaps," not "chaps."

These are the leather pants with no seat in them, and they were invented by the old early Vaqueros. They protected a rider from cactus, brush, weather, horse kicks and bites, falls, rope burns, and many other perils that were part of the cowboy life.

When Mexico broke away from Spain in 1821, twelve years later the new republic took the mission range away from the Spanish Padres, and holdings were then eagerly grabbed by private Rancheros. They were the first real cattle Barons of the West.

The Vaqueros came immediately to full flower, as they were hired by the land Barons. No longer "peons," they now commanded a princely salary of up to $14 per month. Their clothing became more decorative, and their saddles began to flash with silver ornamentation. As he worked the prickly desert brush land of the south, gathering cattle every day, it was to be expected that "chaparejos" would evolve and come into use.

There are three basic styles of chaps with many variations as to added extras and designs that may decorate a pair. The earliest style was the "shotguns." They were often called "leggings" by the American cowboy. The negative side to them was that they were very time consuming to put on and take off. If the man did not begin his day with them being put on first thing in the morning, but later in the day had a need for them, he would have to take off his boots and spurs, put the leggings on, then reverse the whole procedure when he no longer needed them, or at the end of his day. It made the use of the "leggings" or "shotguns" somewhat of a nuisance to him, and I am certain the protection was carefully weighed against the necessity at times.

Necessity soon invented the next style, called "batwings" simply because that is what they resembled. With closures down the sides for easy on and off, the legs were extended to a roomy wide "wing" which also served to cover more of a man's saddle for protection.

These were generally constructed of smooth leather, and soon evolved into quite ornamental dressing with bi-color leather and fancy tie conchos. Sometimes even large initials of either the owner or the ranch he worked for were added to the legs. With the jingle of his spurs, and the wide, decorative batwing chaps on, the cowboy cut quite a figure in early days, and still does in every rodeo today!

The third basic style, called "woolies" are actually a form of "shotguns" with the hair side out. They are a little more difficult to find for the collector today, for several reasons. Being made of hair, they were very susceptible to moths, mice, mold, and other deterioration. Also, they were only used by the cowboys in the North Country, where the greatest protection needed most of the year was warmth. Quite naturally there were probably less in number actually made for the working cowboy.

Woolies soon began to sport colors as the hair was dyed in various shades and thereby gave the cowboy some form of unique and individual appearance. Some of the hair-side-out leather that was used came from sheep, seals, angora goats, buffalo, elk, cattle, and even dog.

In an old 1903 Garcia Catalogue, a pair of woolies could be purchased for as little as $14, with Dog Hair woolies fetching the whole sum of $12 and Sealskin bringing $15. Twenty years later, those same chaps were bringing $27 and $32.

Today, in one of the largest Western Auctions in the country, one pair of woolies sold for $4,400! So it is a fact that the rare and hard to find woolies can certainly fetch a sizeable sum in today's collector circles. I would be remiss if I did not mention condition here. As with anything, Woolie chaps, or for that matter, any other style, must be in at least good condition and still holding all together to bring the large price tags.

I would suggest if you have a pair of woolies in your collection, pack them with moth balls, and in sealed storage if possible. As for the smooth leather chaps, they can be treated as any other leather item, with special attention to mice protection. If they require it, they can be cleaned with saddle soap, but I would use caution here. The original wear showing on a pair of chaps is considered highly desirable.

Fringed cowhide, marked "J.M. Capriola Co.". They are called "chinks" because of the length. *Courtesy Paul and Marlene Snider.* $300-400

Beautiful ornately embroidered charro shotgun chaps. *Courtesy Paul and Marlene Snider.* $800-1200

Marked "George Lawrence" fancy studded batwings with 20 German silver tie conchos, outside pockets, snaps marked "G.L.Co". These chaps are very old and in pristine condition. *Courtesy Paul and Marlene Snider.* $2000-3000

Slick cowhide leather shotgun chaps, with very unique spur shank holes. *Courtesy Paul and Marlene Snider.* $700-800

Latigo leather chaps with carved acorns and oak leaves on belt section, the chaps are a Charlie Baker original. *Courtesy Paul and Marlene Snider.* $600-800

Diamond overlays marked "Hamley and Co., Pendleton, Oregon" number 8823. "WF Brand-Special"...hand tooled belt. *Courtesy Paul and Marlene Snider.* $1200-1500

Smooth leather batwings, made by Hamley and Co. Pendleton, Oregon. They are number 9555, a "97-Special" in size 33. *Courtesy Paul and Marlene Snider.* $800-1000

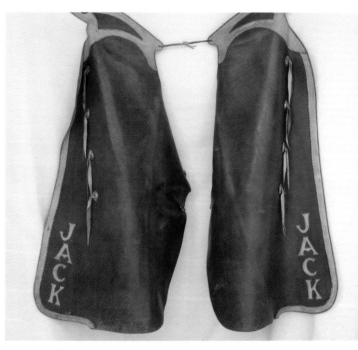

Ray Holes, Grangeville, Idaho, is the maker of chaps, they are smooth batwings and are custom, one of a kind. *Courtesy Jack Snider.* $800-1000

Marked "George Lawrence" with over 200 studs, the fancy studded chaps also have inside pockets. They are old, rare, and very unique. *Courtesy Paul and Marlene Snider.* $3500-3800

Marked "Visalia, San. Fran. Ca." they are batwings with ornate overlays at the borders. 1200 nickel silver spots decorate this pair. Outside pockets, they are very desirable and in wonderful condition. *Courtesy Paul and Marlene Snider.* $3500-5000

Marked "Visalia", they are hand tooled shotguns with fancy fringe and are unused, in never worn condition. *Courtesy Paul and Marlene Snider.* $3000-3500

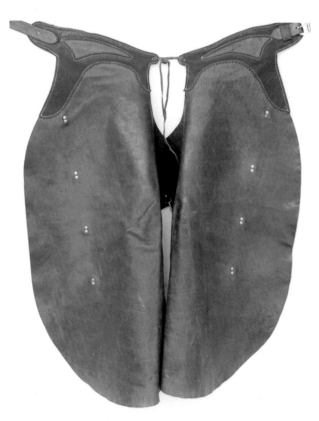

Ray Holes, Grangeville, Idaho, built the smooth leather, working chaps. Mr. Holes is now deceased, and the cowboy world misses his great talent. *Courtesy Paul and Marlene Snider.* $300-500

Horseshoe studded batwings, they are attributed to H.T. Hyser from 1890-1920. *Courtesy Larry and Aileen Fisher.* $1200-1500

Early 1885 George Lawrence shotguns, smooth leather with outside pockets, the chaps are in excellent condition. Note basket weave belt, and fancy pocket stitching. *Courtesy Paul and Marlene Snider.* $3500-5000

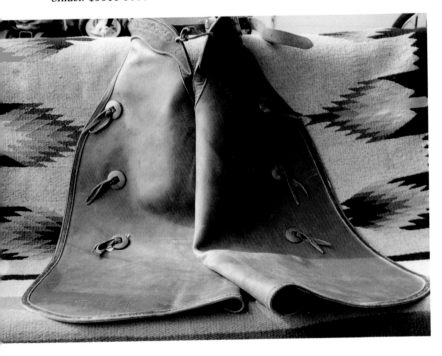

Smooth leather batwings, marked "4F" brand, Montana c. 1940. *Courtesy Larry and Aileen Fisher.* $350-450

These very old smooth leather shotguns are constructed with the early style of leggings. *Overton Collection.* $300-400

Chaps are smooth leather, outside pockets, made by George Lawrence, they belonged to Alice Anderson's Grandfather; "F.A. Jennings" Moscow, Idaho. *Courtesy Alice Jennings-Anderson.* $800-1000

Yellow woolies, made for a little girl. They have fringed legs, and are quite exceptional. *Courtesy Paul and Marlene Snider.* $600-700

Child size black woolies, with basket weave stamped leather belt, the chaps have no name. *Courtesy Paul and Marlene Snider.* $300-400

Dark brown woolies made for a youngster, they have hand carved leather belt. *Courtesy Paul and Marlene Snider.* $300-400

Golden colored woolies, a very desirable and novel color, they are in excellent condition. *Courtesy Paul and Marlene Snider.* $750-850

Very unusual red woolies, they are marked "B.B.81" with basket weave tooled leather belt. *Courtesy Paul and Marlene Snider.* $1000-2000

The chaps are marked "G.S. Garcia, Elko, Nev.", the belt is done in hand carved roses, the batwing legs are hair side out cowhide. *Courtesy Paul and Marlene Snider.* $3500-5000

Wild rose pattern on hand carved belt, the woolies are black, and are unmarked. *Courtesy Paul and Marlene Snider.* $1000-1200

These unique brown and white woolies are from Clark Saddlery, Portland, Oregon. *Courtesy Paul and Marlene Snider.* $2000-2500

Dark brown angora woolies, they are marked "Clark, Portland." *Courtesy Paul and Marlene Snider.* $1000-1200

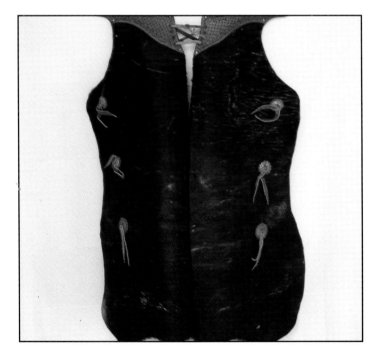

Batwing steerhide with hair side out, they have six tie conchos and a basket weave tooled belt. *Courtesy Paul and Marlene Snider.* $700-800

Black woolies, they are attributed to Miles City Saddlery because of the particular basket weave stamping on the belt. *Courtesy Paul and Marlene Snider.* $1700-2000

Ladies' red woolies, they have been patched, and are very rare and difficult to find. *Courtesy Paul and Marlene Snider.* $700-800

Black woolies…"Britches Shotguns", with the popular basket weave stamping on belt. *Courtesy Paul and Marlene Snider.* $1000-1200

Basket weave belt with attractive studs make this pair of woolies unique and very desirable. They are unmarked. *Courtesy Paul and Marlene Snider.* $1200-1500

Marked "Miles City", black woolies with basket weave belt. *Courtesy Paul and Marlene Snider.* $2500-3000

Marked "Nell E. Thorell, Winn. Nev.-Costume and Hair Shop". The woolies are rare white ones with a basket weave belt. *Courtesy Paul and Marlene Snider.* $2000-2500

Dark brown woolies marked "Clark, Portland, Or". *Courtesy Paul and Marlene Snider.* $1200-1500

Desert rose pattern on belt, they are a most unusual and rare orange color. *Courtesy Paul and Marlene Snider.* $1500-1700

Basket weave belt, chaps are a cream color, unmarked woolies. *Courtesy Paul and Marlene Snider.* $1500-1700

Black woolies with hand carved leather belt, they are attributed to "Porter". *Courtesy Paul and Marlene Snider.* $1500-1750

Bi-color "cherapes", smooth leather lined. Cherapes were usually draped behind the saddle for decoration. *Courtesy Paul and Marlene Snider.* $800-900

"Cherapes" with tooled border in leather piece. *Courtesy Paul and Marlene Snider.* $700-800

CHAPTER SIX

BITS

It is said that the Scythians, Caucasian Nomads, who ranged between North Turkistan and South Russia in 4000 to 5000 B.C., had devised crude bridle bits, making the earliest known bit date back a considerable amount of time.

The bridle bit, like so many other items of cowboy equipment, was first brought to this continent by the Spanish Conquistadores. It would be safe to say that most of the very early Spanish bits were a crude version of what we now recognize as chilenos and spades. Without much imagination involved, it would be easy to picture the early use of those first bits. Very inhumane in structure and usage, a horse was probably lucky if he survived a one day battle, because if a spear didn't get him, his rider's hand and a cruel bit would! Since horses were regarded by the Spanish as simple "War Tools," if a jaw on a horse was broken and he died, there was always another horse to take his place.

Bit construction and design was refined greatly in the following years of California Missions and during the period of Rancheros and Vaqueros. The Vaquero loved his horse a little more than his ancestors did, and the metal forges at the Missions burned hot with new innovations and ornamentation. Some of the better known bit designs that came out of that era fall into the category of the Santa Barbara spade, the Las Crucas, and the silver mounted chileno or ring bit.

Most of those early Mission made bits were quite a lot heavier with thicker cheek plates than what we see today, and were a cast metal, created with a sand cast method, rather than the forged methods later used. There are very few of the old Mission made bits around today. Bits that were constructed with the cast method were very difficult to repair when needed, and because of this many nice old bits fell by the way.

When August Beurmann first began to build bits in this country, he followed the old Mission methods and produced some beautiful examples of Mission style, cast or molded bits.

There are six basic styles, or categories, that bridle bits fall into: Chilenos, spades, half breeds, ports, Military, and snaffle. Bits are usually assessed and categorized by the type of mouth piece they carry.

CHILENO, OR RING BIT

Generally looked upon as the premium bit in the collector world, simply because they are unique, rare, and difficult to find. Chilenos have a complete circled ring in the mouth piece section that encircles the horse's lower jaw. Without that ring section, the bit would be a half breed, for that is how they are constructed. The chileno is also considered by many today as being a cruel or inhumane type of bit, which is not entirely true. Designed by the Spanish, it is true that they could be very cruel and in the hands of a careless reinsman, tear up a horse's jaw quite easily. However, a good reinsman could have excellent control and results using them. The best rule of thumb here is "A bit is only as cruel as the man who holds the reins."

We once owned a big dappled grey quarter horse who was so well trained and educated he would bow upon command, and Mr. Overton rode him with a silver mounted ring bit that made both man and horse a real show stopper! We had him for several years and when he left our hands, he was flown to Hawaii, but he had worn the chileno often and was never harmed once. It simply comes back down to "the man who holds the reins." Adjusting the head stall on a bridle with a chileno in it is always a crucial factor here.

Chased metal ring bit with sterling silver caps, it is in pristine condition and attributed to Larios. *Overton Collection.* $500-700

Detail of "kissing bird" motif from Main and Winchester ring bit. *Overton Collection.*

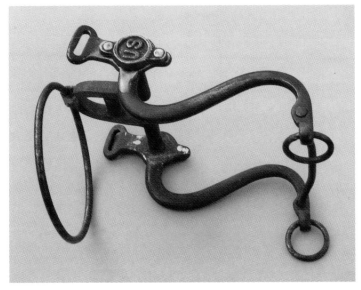

U.S. Cavalry ring bit, in excellent condition. *Overton Collection.* $500-700

Detail of concho on Main and Winchester ring bit. *Overton Collection.*

Ring bit pictured in Main and Winchester catalogue 1897, it is in pristine condition. *Overton Collection.* $1800-2000

SPADES

A spade bit has a spade shaped mouth piece with cricket in it, and generally copper wrapped side rails running from the spade to the cheek plates. The cricket in the spade acts as a kind of "pacifier" to the horse.

Spade bits come in various forms of spade mouth piece; straight spade, spoon spade, low spade, and double cricketed spade, each are self descriptive. Spades also come in solid or loose jaw design.

There are so many various cheek plates that have been done in spade bits, it is almost impossible to list them all. However, a few styles that bear special recognition are the Santa Barbara, always recognized by the classic hole in the very ornate cheek plate; the La Cruz or Las Crucas spade, recognized by usually one large concho and a very straight, slender shank that is ornamented with silver inlays; and the Colorado cheek plate, which was a large open, elongated heart shape. Pistols, lady legs (gal legs), and snakes on cheek plates are also very popular and desirable styles.

Mexican ring bit with unique double cricket and silver spots, c. 1910. *Courtesy Roy and Jeanenne Williams.* $300-400

Old Santa Barbara spade bit, it has U.S. Shield engraved on cheek plates. Maker unknown. *Overton Collection.* $1200-1500

Old Mission spade bit, in original condition except for added patina, it is, of course unmarked, as no marks were ever used by early Missions. *Overton Collection.* $3000-4000

Detail of concho on old Mission spade. *Overton Collection.*

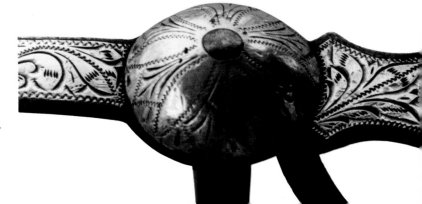

Mike Morales is the maker of this old spade bit, it has ornate "kissing birds" and large silver concho. Bit is not in good condition, missing the side rails in mouth piece. *Overton Collection.* $200-400

Ed Connell is the maker of this bit, which was sold through Carroll Saddlery in McNeal, Arizona. Ed Connel marked his bits with an "E.C." and a star, however his "C" most often looked like a "G" and has caused many collectors today to mistake his work for other makers. This bit was purchased from Ed when brand new, by an Overton family member many years ago, and has never been put in a horse's mouth. *Overton Collection.* $2000-2500

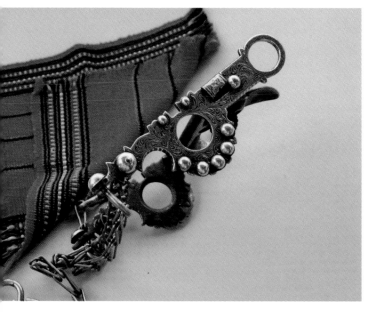

Old Santa Barbara spade bit, in very excellent condition, it is the classic Santa Barbara cheek plate, and attributed to Garcia. *Overton Collection.* $2000-2500

Detail of Santa Barbara spoon spade bit, attributed to Garcia.

Detail of Ed Connell Texas star bit. *Overton Collection.*

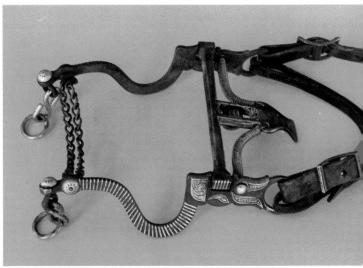

Mike Morales spade bit, with "kissing bird" motif. *Overton Collection.* $700-1000

Ed Connell from Carroll Saddlery in McNeal, Arizona, is the maker of this fine old spade bit. It is loose jawed, and in excellent condition. *Courtesy Bob and Judy Bertsch.* $1200-1500

Spade bit made by Les Garcia. It has a double cricket in the mouth piece, and is in pristine condition, never used. *Overton Collection.* $1000-1200

Detail of Les Garcia spade and the double crickets.

HALF BREEDS

The half breed is just what its name implies: half spade, half port in a modified version of both. This style mouth piece incorporates the use of a cricket, as does the spade, but has a bent port shape also. Once the design caught on, it rapidly became the most popular style and soon replaced the spade in many a cowboy bridle!

The cheek plates can vary greatly, but almost any style or design that was ever done in a spade was eventually also done in a half breed. Some of the old catalogues, such as Main and Winchester, 1897, offered the spade and the half breed in identical cheek plate designs with comparable prices.

The cricket in a mouth piece is always a good measure of age and usage. If the hole inside the cricket is large and shows a smooth "wearing," it is old and has been used a lot. If the cricket has its original small hole and is well grooved inside the hole, the bit has not been used very much. These are good things to remember when trying to determine the age of a half breed, or spade.

Mike Morales is the maker, it is the chevron design he quite often used. *Overton Collection.* $600-1000

Maker unknown, it is an old half breed bit with silver overlays. *Overton Collection.* $200-400

Mike Morales is the maker of this half breed, it is in excellent condition c. 1910 *Overton Collection.* $700-1000

Attributed to August Buermann, the half breed is in excellent condition with original rein chains. *Overton Collection.* $300-600

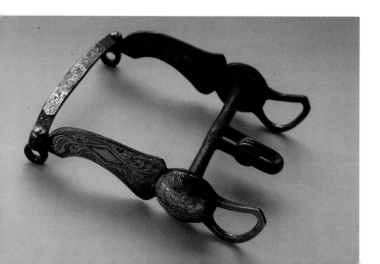

Half breed made in prison, completely wrapped in silver with beautiful engraving. *Overton Collection.* $1200-1400

August Buermann "DAISY" bit, it is in lovely condition, and the "DAISY" is very visible. It says "Buermann Patd" on the mouth piece. *Overton Collection.* $700-1000

Les Garcia is the maker, the bit is a classic long shank with many small conchos as overlay on top of the sterling silver mounting. *Overton Collection.* $800-1000

Detail of the August Buermann "DAISY" stamp in cheek plate. *Overton Collection.*

Detail of the Les Garcia half breed showing all the many little inlays and overlays of silver on cheek plates. *Overton Collection.*

August Buermann "DAISY" with a changed mouth piece. *Overton Collection.* $500-700

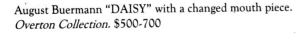

Richard Pettijohn is the maker of this ox shoe half breed. It is unique and one of a kind. *Overton Collection.* $500-700

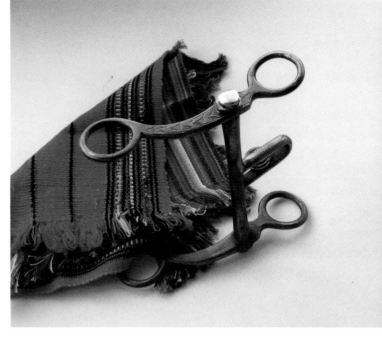

North and Judd half breed, with chased metal and a small sterling silver cap. *Overton Collection.* $200-400

Low spade with leaf design, attributed to Walla Walla, Washington, State Prison. *Overton Collection.* $400-700

Attributed to Mike Morales, the half breed is in excellent condition. *Overton Collection.* $700-1000

Detail of "kissing bird" design on the Mike Morales half breed. *Overton Collection.*

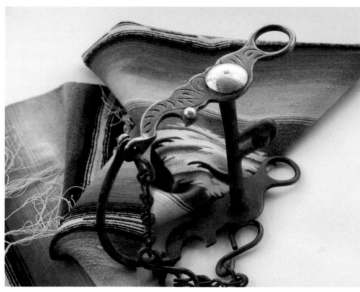

Iron chased "flying bird" half breed bit, maker unknown. *Overton Collection.* $200-500

Attributed to Visalia, the half breed bit is in pristine condition and has beautiful engraving. *Overton Collection.* $300-500

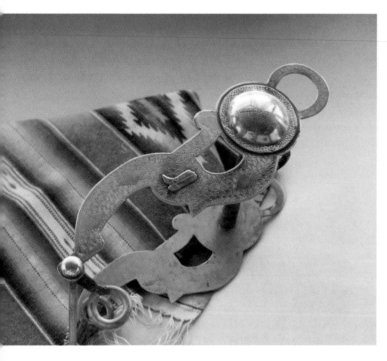

Maker unknown, the bit has nice old patina and is very fine work with 32 pieces of inlay, and lovely old conchos. The fine tuned mouth piece has been used extensively. Possibly Mission made. *Overton Collection.* $800-1000

This half breed was made in the early 1920s in the State Prison at Salem, Oregon. The little overlay of boot makes it unique. *Overton Collection.* $400-600

Half breed is made by Vogt, it is a lovely bit with engraved copper Mona Lisa mouth piece and unusual cactus flower cheek plate. *Overton Collection.* $500-700

Attributed to Garcia, it has a Salinas mouth piece in it, and is the eagle design. *Overton Collection.* $1000-1500

"G.S. Garcia, Elko, NV." c. 1910, snake bit, a very classic design of the snake cheek plates, a splendid example of craftsmanship. *Courtesy Paul and Marlene Snider.* $2000-2500

Mike Morales is the maker of this nice old half breed bit with "chevron" design, c. 1910. *Courtesy Paul and Marlene Snider.* $800-1000

Marked "E. Garcia" the bit is a lovely contemporary half breed with a Salinas mouth piece and "half moon" design. The heart overlay is rather unusual and attractive. *Courtesy William Scott Deatherage.* $350-550

"F.M. Stern" half breed bit with cricket missing, but has beautiful large "sand dollar" conchos, and engraving with one large "bird head" on cheek plate down towards slobber bar. *Courtesy Paul and Marlene Snider.* $1200-1500

"Three hearts" is the cheek plate design, the half breed is actually called a "frog" mouth piece. Maker is Fleming. *Overton Collection.* $500-700

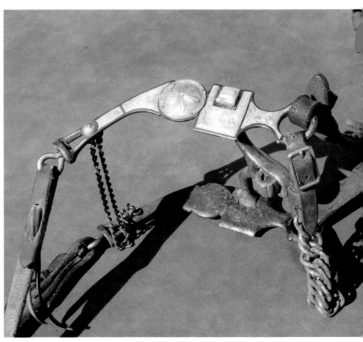

Marked "A. Tietjen" bit has a Mona Lisa mouth piece with Colorado cheek plates, and is in excellent condition. Bit is being used today. *Courtesy Roy and Jeanenne Williams.* $500-700

Pistol bit, copper cricket with a Salinas mouth piece, the bit is unmarked, but has nice silver overlays. *Courtesy Larry and Aileen Fisher.* $900-1500

Bit is a classic Santa Barbara cheek plate it is unmarked but in lovely condition, with Salinas mouth piece. *Courtesy Roy and Jeanenne Williams.* $300-500

Half breed is made by "Diablo", it has six silver overlay spots and a loose jaw. Very nice silver bit it is in a working cowboy's bridle. *Courtesy Bob and Judy Bertsch.* $350-550

PORTS AND GRAZERS

A port bit has a simple bent bar mouth piece. Some are low ports where the actual bend is slight, some are high ports, where the bend is quite high and pronounced. Often termed "curb" bits, most ports are of fairly simple construction and yet often times very ornamented and fancy in decorative silver overlays and inlays.

The port or curb bit was the natural choice for the cowboy in daily use. It was easy to put on and take off, and it would generally fit most animals.

The grazer bit is a short shanked version of the port, whereby the short side pieces allow the horse to graze while wearing the bit.

MILITARY

Very early on, most Military bits were versions or copies of the European ports with straight slender cheeks and generally a low to medium port as mouth piece. During the Civil War, Military bit design advanced as foundries in the North and South mass produced bits.

The Shoemaker bit came on the scene in 1874, and its famous "S" shank design has often been used and embellished by latter day cowboys.

Military bits have been very enduring and constitute a specialized interest in collecting today. Officer's bits were somewhat more ornamented than regular issue bits, and are very desirable. There were even a few ring bits made for the Military, but they are fairly rare. One of the earliest Military bit makers was August Buermann.

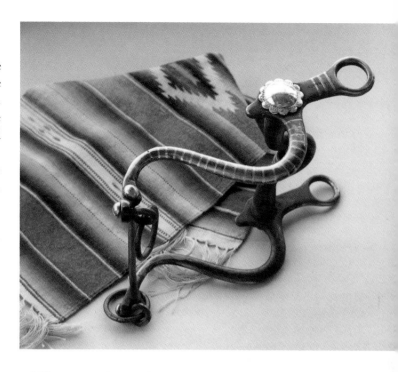

Military issue, this port bit has contemporary inlays. *Overton Collection.* $100-300

Low port bit with silver engraved overlay, it is prison made attributed to Walla Walla, Washington State Prison. *Overton Collection.* $200-500

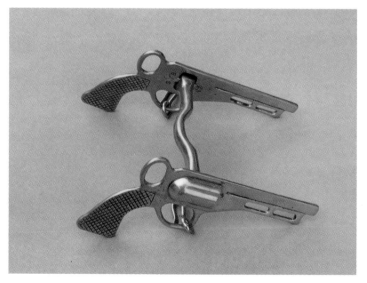

Pistol bit is all German silver with "S.B." marked in it. Sorry I must leave it a mystery for you readers to solve, but it is splendid example of the pistol design. *Courtesy Larry and Aileen Fisher.* $750-1000

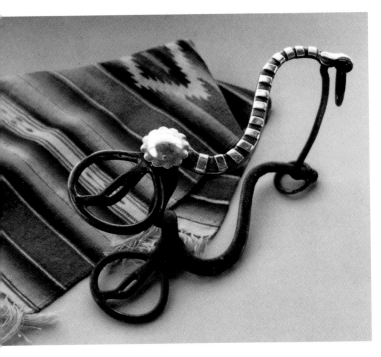

Shoemaker is the bit and it was U.S. Cavalry issue, but in latter days it became popular for cowboys to "dress up" the Military bits and use them. *Overton Collection.* $500-700

Both bits are Military issue; on the left an original Shoemaker, and on the right is a Civil War issue. *Overton Collection.* $300-500 each

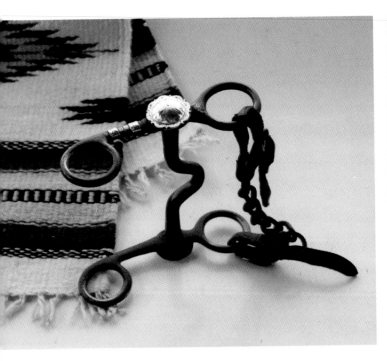

Kelly Bros. short shanked grazer bit with a silver overlay. *Overton Collection.* $300-500

North and Judd little grazer bit with a medium port mouth piece, and silver mounted overlays. *Overton Collection.* $200-300

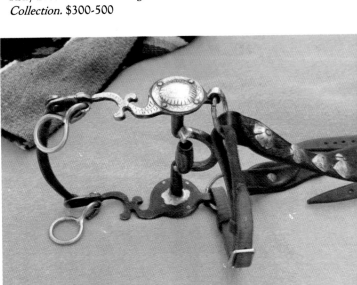

The card suit head stall is by Charlie Baker, the port mouth piece with roller is a bit made by Gene Prater. *Courtesy Bob and Judy Bertsch.* $500-600

86

Early Shoemaker bit Military issue, in very good shape. *Courtesy Bob and Judy Bertsch.* $225-250

North and Judd pony bit it has a low port mouth piece in it. *Courtesy Bob and Judy Bertsch.* $50-75

Old high port mouth piece this bit is blacksmith made. *Courtesy Bob and Judy Bertsch.* $125-150

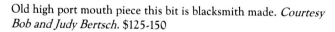

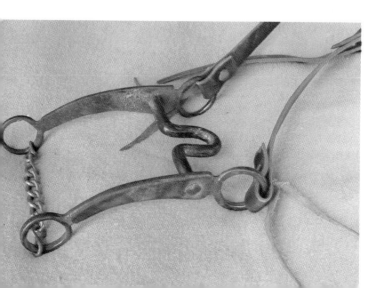

Unknown maker the bit is a port with a ring and roller. It has interesting cheek plates and is quite unique. *Courtesy Bob and Judy Bertsch.* $450-550

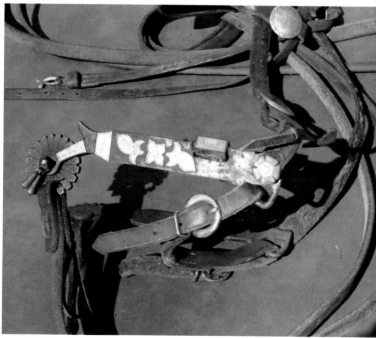

Robert Campbell from Texas, made this "spur" bit with spur cheek plates and jingle bobs, it has a low port mouth piece, is number 13 of 25. Very rare and unusual. *Courtesy Roy and Jeanenne Williams.* $500-600

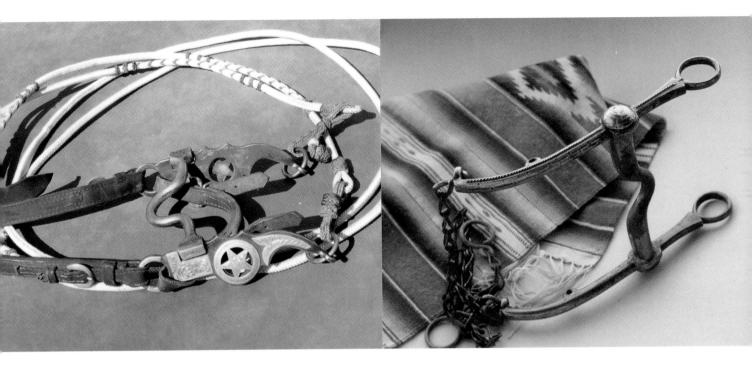

Robert Campbell loose jawed with the Texas Star motif on cheek plates, it is a medium port mouth piece. *Courtesy Roy and Jeanenne Williams.* $600-700

Mexican made, it has a fine silver rope overlay and greek key design on the conchos. It was made with a low port mouth piece that has some copper. *Overton Collection.* $200-400

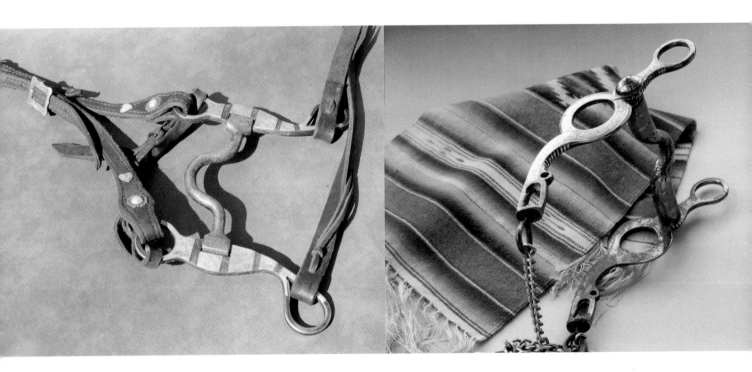

Loose jawed port made by Robert Campbell, it has some Visalia silver on head stall and is a working cowboy's rig. *Courtesy Roy and Jeanenne Williams.* $450-650

Mexican made, the bit has nice balance and lovely silver cheek plates, it is a low port. *Overton Collection.* $300-500

Prison made low port, the bit is detailed with wild roses engraved into the silver and is an altogether pleasing design. *Overton Collection.* $400-600

Hand forged medium port bit with silver inlays and overlays. *Overton Collection.* $300-500

North and Judd with the "anchor" brand, it has silver inlay, and silver conchos. *Overton Collection.* $100-300

Crockett/Renalde medium port copper wrapped mouth piece with diamond silver overlays. *Overton Collection.* $100-300

August Beurmann is the maker of this globe bit with high port mouth piece. *Overton Collection.* $100-200

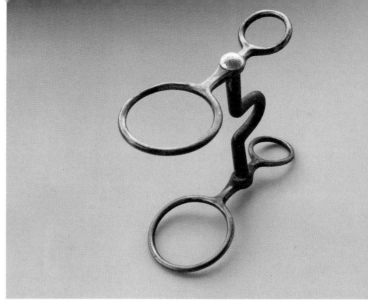

Unmarked globe bit with high port mouth piece. It has a silver concho on the sides, most likely an addition. *Overton Collection.* $200-300

SNAFFLES

Snaffle bits were another European contribution to this country, and are still widely used in horse breaking and training today. The snaffle is one of the easier bits to get a horse used to wearing, and therefore works well to get a young horse used to the feel of a bit in its mouth. They come in a wide variety of sizes and styles, and are still being manufactured and marketed today.

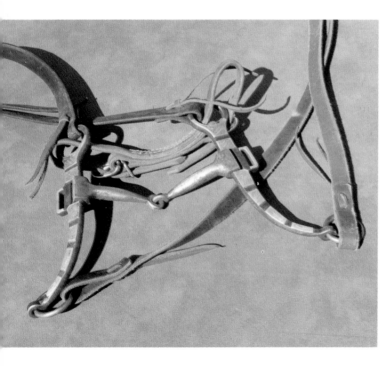

Robert Campbell cowboy snaffle bit, it has a unique design with silver overlays. *Courtesy Roy and Jeanenne Williams.* $600-800

Three snaffle bits, each with a somewhat different design. *Overton Collection.* $25 each

CHAPTER SEVEN
SPURS

America has long had a kind of special romance with the cowboy spur. Whether it was the jingle sound that seemed to follow the cowboy's feet everywhere he went and produced, seemingly, his own special music; or perhaps just the actual appearance of a boot with spurs on the heels, whatever its source, we all love spurs. They seem to hold a kind of "Western Charm" that no other piece of cowboy Equipment quite equals.

The root of this romance with spurs came by way of a Spanish Conquistador named Cortez who introduced the Espuela Grande, or "Great Spur" to the New World in 1520. It had huge eight and nine inch rowels, large "jingle bobs," or pajados, as they were called, and quite ornate heel bands. A very impressive spur all in all.

Mexican Vaqueros were still wearing the Great Spur of their ancestors in the 1850s. Then several transitional models or designs finally ushered in the classic period of Mexican spur making which extended from about the 1860s into the 20th century.

There are five basic classes or categories that spurs fall into: Mexican Vaquero, California Style, Texas Style, Great Plains, and Prison Made. Taking each one separately, and touching on some very basic information as space allows, they are as follows:

MEXICAN VAQUERO

The very first thing to remember here is that all spurs evolved from their Mexican roots and therefore a great respect for any Mexican made spur should somehow exist. We all tend to overlook sometimes the more recent South of the Border examples in modern day spur making and their value. However, there are spurs being made today in Mexico that are evidence of talent and craftsmanship reminiscent of the old Masters and certainly a lovely addition to anyone's collection. They are contemporary, yes, but certainly desirable.

While it is true there are some very crude examples being made in the charro spur style that perhaps are being aimed at a tourist type trade and market, there are also some very nice California style spurs being built and sold today.

The large rowelled charro Parade spur can still be seen at Mexican Fiestas and celebrations, and are very similar to the original Espuela Grande of Cortez's time, but these are difficult to find.

Spurs made in the Zacateca area of Mexico in the 1880s still displayed the large eight inch rowels.

Mexican spurs are very rarely, if ever, marked with makers name. Most of the California style come with pajados or "jingle bobs" which make them attractive to some collectors.

Mexican "charro" spurs, they picture a full body horse on heel bands. *Courtesy Phyllis A. Shovelski.* $300-400

Detail of horse on heel band of "charro" spurs.

CALIFORNIA STYLE

California Style spurs are generally recognized by their two piece construction, ornate silver overlays and inlays, fairly large rowels, and oft times double heel chains. They quite naturally exhibit the Vaquero and Mexican influence both in flair, style, and ornamentation.

California Style spurs were produced by many various early spur makers and Master Artisans. Some of the more noted ones are include August Buermann, Oscar Crockett, Juan Estrada, José Figueroa, G.S. Garcia, Raphael Guiterrez, A. Larios, Mike Morales, North and Judd, and the list goes on. Each one of these Master spur makers carved his own name into the annals of history with every marked spur he ever built.

There are many unmarked spurs out there folks, but most are "marked" by many other things just as recognizable, such as style, shape, and engraving.

Every pair of old California Style spurs has passed the acid test of time, and has now become a part of the history of the West. They are highly desirable and collectible in any collector's estimation.

Small pair of California drop shank spurs with one leather missing. The one leather is most likely original, c. 1800s. *Courtesy Marlin Pool.* $150-175

Marked with "Qualey Bros", these spurs are single mounted with double buttons and are beautifully engraved. *Courtesy Paul and Marlene Snider.* $5000-6000

California style spurs, they are Crockett blanks with Ed Bolin silver mounting. Parade spurs with "clover leaf" design, c. 1930s. *Courtesy Paul and Marlene Snider.* $3000-3500

Silver shield design spurs with 28 point rowels, August Buermann's mark with a star, c. 1900. *Courtesy Paul and Marlene Snider.* $3500-5000

Marked "G.S. Garcia" they are silver shield design c. 1900-1910, and in wonderful condition. *Courtesy Paul and Marlene Snider.* $3500-4000

Spurs are the California style, marked with "G.S. Garcia, Elko, Nv." in his earliest oval shaped mark which dates them to pre-1900. They are in pristine condition, and very rare. *Courtesy Paul and Marlene Snider.* $10000-12000

August Buermann California drop shanks, most likely made for a lady. They also have the early Harpham Bros. leathers, collectable straps themselves. *Overton Collection.* $800-1000

Detail of engraving on the August Buermann spurs

August Buermann chased metal California drop shank style with original rowels. They are in nice condition with contemporary leathers. *Courtesy William Scott Deatherage.* $550-750

Early California style single, it is for the left boot—do you have right? *Overton Collection.* $150-350

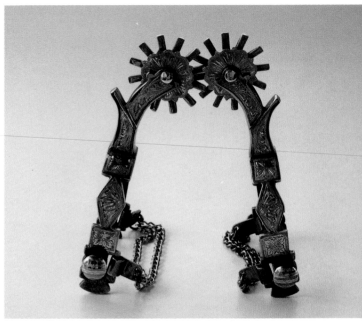

Contemporary California style marked with "E.C.". *Overton Collection.* $800-1000

Spurs are marked with August Buermann's mark, they are in wonderful condition and have been in the Sears family since the first of this century. *Courtesy Orvil Sears Jr.* $2000-3000

Garcia "dandy" design California style spurs with rowel shields. *Overton Collection.* $500-700

The classic "snake" design on heel bands, these spurs are marked with a star like Buermann's with an additional "V" in heel bands. *Courtesy William Scott Deatherage.* $1000-1200

Spurs are marked "E. Garcia" they are a contemporary rendition of the original Garcia "dandy" design. *Courtesy William Scott Deatherage.* $300-500

There is an interesting story behind this unmatched pair of spurs. They belonged to F.A. Jennings, Moscow, Idaho, who used them regularly as a working ranch owner and cowboy. They have been in the family for three generations. The one on the left is North and Judd, the one on the right is August Buermann. *Courtesy Alyce Jennings Anderson.* $150-250

August Buermann California drop shank style spurs, showing some age corrosion but are classic representation of the style. *Courtesy Phyllis A. Shovelski.* $275-375

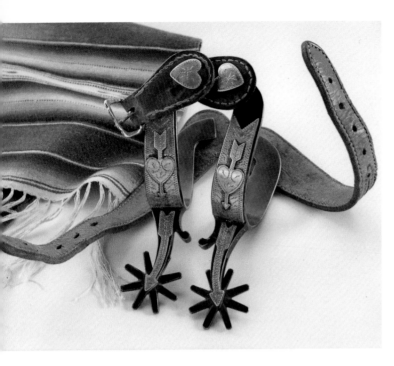

Single spur, August Buermann drop shank in California style. *Courtesy Roy and Jeanenne Williams.* $50-75

The "arrow" shank design has always been a favorite with spur makers. These were made by Ed Lawrence, Alzada, Montana. *Courtesy Phyllis A. Shovelski.* $400-500

California style with nice "barrel" chap guards and large 20 point rowels, they are made by R. Williams and are one of a kind. Large one and a half inch concho on leathers is sterling silver. *Courtesy Roy and Jeanenne Williams.* $1200-1500

Marked with North and Judds "anchor" brand behind inside spur button. They are chased metal California drop shanks. *Courtesy Phyllis A. Shovelski.* $400-600

Contemporary Garcia California style with very nice engraving on silver. *Overton Collection.* $600-800

Contemporary Garcias, these spurs have the very desirable "moon and star" design and are ornamented with beautiful engraved silver. *Overton Collection.* $700-900

Maker is Les Garcia, the spurs have over 200 separate tiny inlays in each spur, rowels are inlaid also. *Overton Collection.* $700-1000

California style spurs they are marked with "E.C.". *Overton Collection.* $500-700

Spurs are Les Garcia's with nice little silver concho overlays and beautiful chap guards and rowel shields. Conchos on leathers are also sterling silver. *Overton Collection.* $700-1000

TEXAS STYLE

Texas Style spurs are often recognized by their single piece construction, sometimes a simple but unique design on shanks and heel bands, rarely having chap guards, and seldom blued. They have a more "sturdy" and "Practical" look to them with somewhat less decoration than the California Style.

From a cowboy's point of view, these were the spurs to have for actual working use. They generally have smaller, more useful type rowels in them, and they were an easy on, easy off type spur

Some Masters at the Texas Style of spur making were: John R. McChesney, Pascal M. Kelly, Bob Boone, Joe Bianchi, J.O. Bass, and Garcia. There are many more that I have not listed for lack of space, but needless to say, in the world of Western Collectibles, each and every one is highly regarded.

GREAT PLAINS STYLE

Spurs of the Great Plains (sometimes termed "Northern Plains") style are a form of both California and Texas style combined. With some features of both, they became a style all their own. They are usually a one piece construction with silver overlays and inlays. They are often decorated on both shank and heel band. They have larger rowels than the Texas style, as a general rule.

Sometimes it's a tough call to make when looking at a Great Plains style. There were a lot of blacksmiths, or small local shops making the Great Plains style and some

of these have the same amount of "fit and finish" as the Master makers' work.

Some notable Masters of the Great Plains style were: J.R. McChesney, Robert Causey, Oscar Crockett, Phillips and Guiterrez, Rex Schnitger, August Buermann, Dee Boone, Ed Bohlin, and North and Judd.

PRISON MADE

Prison made spurs have a special attraction all their own in collecting circles. For one thing, it is very difficult to determine whether or not in fact they were made in prison. Very few were stamped or marked, and when they were it was in a very vague way with either the inmate's prison number, or perhaps initials. Most were left completely unmarked.

Strange as it may seem, there were Masters even in this class of spurs, and their work has come to special light and recognition in these latter days. They are: John Cox, John Peoples, Carl Erickson, E.H. McKinney, Robert Baldwin, among others.

When determining if they may be prison made spurs, look for unusual rowels, sometimes very unorthodox, and decorative, generally an affinity to either the Texas style or Great Plains style in shape.

There were several prisons that had active, well-fitted metal shops that helped to produce good quality spurs. Some of them were: Canon City, Colorado; Huntsville, Texas; Yuma, Arizona; Walla Walla, Washington; Deer Lodge, Montana; McCallister, Oklahoma; and Salem, Oregon, and I am sure there were others.

Texas style bronc spurs, marked "Crockett" inside the heel band. They have a very nice leaf design and are in pristine condition. *Courtesy Paul and Marlene Snider.* $1500-2000

Stamped "Crockett" inside the heel band, they are some of his very early ones. *Courtesy Paul and Marlene Snider.* $1500-2000

Very unusual brass spurs, they are silver mounted and marked with "E-M" in the heel band. *Courtesy Roy and Jeanenne Williams.* $900-1000

Mike Morales is the maker of these spurs in Texas style, very typical of Mike's work. *Overton Collection.* $1500-2000

Spurs are marked with Crockett-Renalde mark and done nicely in the Texas style. They are in excellent condition and bear contemporary leathers. *Overton Collection.* $500-800

Prison made, attributed to Canon City, Colorado, these spurs are made in Texas style and have Harpham Bros. leathers. *Overton Collection.* $600-800

Texas style spurs marked with Garcia in heel band and have been in Overton family for three generations. Originally they were acquired by trading off a curly haired horse. *Overton Collection.* $2500-3500

Blacksmith or "shop" made, the spurs have nice silver overlays. *Overton Collection.* $300-500

Single spur attributed to McChesney with double heart design. *Courtesy William Scott Deatherage.* $75-100

Marked "Crockett", these spurs have unique rowels that are original, with original leathers as well. *Courtesy Phyllis A. Shovelski.* $500-600

Silver trophy spurs they were won by "Tiny" Bertsch with rawhide covered buckles on the leathers. *Courtesy Bob and Judy Bertsch.* $1000-1500

Unmarked lady legs, most likely to be August Buermann, they have contemporary leathers. *Courtesy William Scott Deatherage.* $1200-1500

Les Garcia spurs with deep engraving on the silver. *Overton Collection.* $300-500

"Rodeo" spurs made by Kelly, they are fairly contemporary, but are no longer in production today. *Overton Collection.* $100-200

Unmarked spurs sold by Carroll Saddlery, McNeal, Arizona, they have been kept in pristine condition, with original leathers. *Overton Collection.* $500-700

The maker of these beautiful spurs with tiny concho overlays is Les Garcia. *Overton Collection.* $500-700

Marked with "Rodeo", these spurs were built by Kelly. *Overton Collection.* $100-200

Spurs are marked "First American" they are built in Aztec, New Mexico. *Overton Collection.* $200-300

Unmarked Texas style spurs with smooth silver buttons and unique rowels. *Overton Collection.* $600-800

August Buermann long shanks with lovely silver engraving and large sterling silver conchos on the leathers. *Overton Collection.* $1500-2000

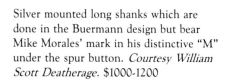

Spurs are unmarked long shanks with "buzz saw-like" rowels, they are possibly Bianchi. *Overton Collection.* $500-800

Silver mounted long shanks which are done in the Buermann design but bear Mike Morales' mark in his distinctive "M" under the spur button. *Courtesy William Scott Deatherage.* $1000-1200

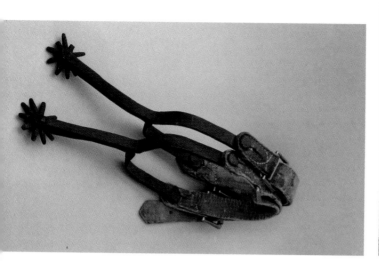

Spurs are hand forged c. late 1800s, they were before rowel guards and most likely used with batwing chaps or woolies. Great Plains. *Courtesy Larry and Aileen Fisher.* $350-400

Spurs made for Tiny Bertsch, Stanfield, Oregon. Lonnie Davis of John Day, Oregon, is the maker. *Courtesy Bob and Judy Bertsch.* $300-500

These are marked "Crockett" with, sadly enough, the silver burned off one spur. Oh, if they could speak! *Courtesy William Scott Deatherage.* $100-150

Marked with "Crockett" these spurs have eagles on the heel bands. *Courtesy Roy and Jeanenne Williams.* $400-500

Star rowelled "arrow shanks", these are marked with the North and Judd anchor. *Courtesy William Scott Deatherage.* $150-200

Crockett working type spurs with nickel silver heart buttons. *Courtesy Bob and Judy Bertsch.* $375-475

CHAPTER EIGHT
GUNS AND KNIVES

The old saying is "God didn't make all men equal, but Colonel Colt did," and one hundred years ago, those words could not have been more true!

All too often, the scales of justice tipped in favor of the man who held the gun, whether it be Colt, Henry, Winchester, or Smith and Wesson. Between cattle rustlers, warring Native Americans, rattlesnakes, and plain old mean-natured thieves, a cowboy was ill-equipped if there was no working firearm within an easy reach!

Where the gunfighter of yesteryear always carefully selected his firearm of preference, that was not always the case of the working trail hand. Sometimes his gun was one passed down from some old frontiersman relative or friend, other times his gun was purchased for one reason only; it was what he could afford, and what he found available.

This particular revolver was carried by many cowboys, some we knew, some we didn't. It is a .41 Colt and been in the Overton family for a very long time. *Overton Collection.* $1200-1500

The very early revolvers in this country were operated with a kind of "make your own" ammunition which consisted of ball, powder, and percussion cap. This lethal combination all too often either fired off neighboring rounds in a kind of domino effect, or even worse, it sometimes just failed entirely. In most cases, where they were loaded with care, they were effective. The development of metal cartridges helped to solve many problems for the man who carried a revolver.

The very famous 1873 Colt "Peacemaker" was not all its name implied in actual usage either. Its short barrel of eight inches or less reduced the power and accuracy greatly. Considered effective at approximately forty yards by an expert marksman, in the absolute turmoil of combat, that figure was reduced by half at least. Because of this, many men added an extra firearm in the way of rifle or shotgun to his arsenal.

In light of the fact that a poor working cowboy generally could afford but one piece, his usual choice (in spite of what is seen in movies) would have been a good carbine carried in a scabbard on his saddle.

One of the best selling rifles in the West was a Winchester .44-.40 model 1873. It boasted an extra rear sight for greater accuracy, and because of its smooth lever action it was excellent for fairly rapid fire that was so often needed. Of course, the Henry .44 caliber was the first practical lever action rifle. Introduced in 1860, it had a range potential of 200 yards, and most likely kicked like a mule!

Since that time, the evolution of the lever action brought the Winchester to the .30 caliber which was very popular with cowboys and still is today. The .30-.30 and both the .30 and .32 made a wonderful lightweight lever action saddle gun, popular with all men making their living in a saddle.

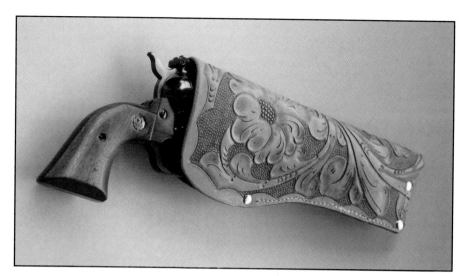

The gun rig is missing its belt part, but the holster itself is in good condition, hand carved leather with a floral design. The revolver is a .357 caliber. *Overton Collection.* $500-700

Colt "Bisley", it is a .44-40 caliber with "stag" grips, and single action. The silver plating is not nickel as one would expect, but true sterling silver and engraved with very ornate engraving. Very beautiful hand gun. *Courtesy Paul and Marlene Snider.* $4000-5000

The revolver is a Scofield, .44 caliber, single action, six shot with a six and one half inch barrel. *Courtesy Paul and Marlene Snider.* $5000-6000

Colt single action "Bisley" Model, it is the "Colt Frontier" six shooter .44 caliber with a seven and one half inch barrel. *Courtesy Paul and Marlene Snider.* $2000-2500

The revolver is a "Colt Frontier" six shooter, .44-40 caliber with fourteen notches filed into the ejector tube, representing that many violent deaths. It has a six and one half inch barrel. *Courtesy Paul and Marlene Snider.* $1500-2000

Colt revolver it is .45 caliber single action, Patd. 1871, it has a four and one half inch barrel. *Courtesy Paul and Marlene Snider.* $2000-2500

This is a black powder .44-40 Colt single action stamped with "U.S." making it an Indian War issue. *Courtesy Paul and Marlene Snider.* $2500-3000

Tim Holt, the Western movie star owned this .38 caliber Colt, the barrel and cylinder have been changed for the movies. "T.H." is under the grips, and it would shoot one to five blanks. Provenance has stayed with it. *Courtesy Paul and Marlene Snider.* $2000-2500

Early black powder .44-40 Colt single action in gun rig with a U.S. Marshal badge, both have been long used. *Courtesy Paul and Marlene Snider.* $3500-4500

Native American beaded holster attributed to Nez Perce, it has a .38 caliber revolver in it with "1-11-1887". *Courtesy Larry and Aileen Fisher.* $1000-1500

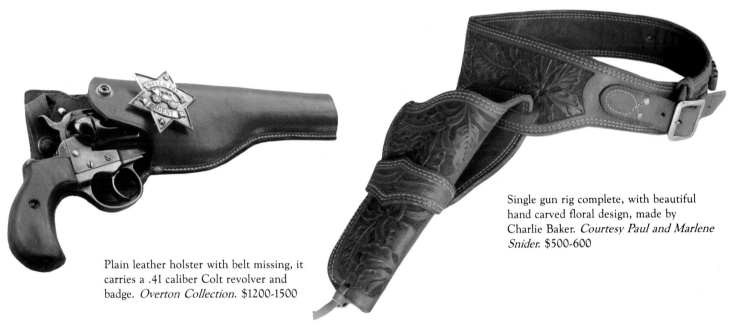

Plain leather holster with belt missing, it carries a .41 caliber Colt revolver and badge. *Overton Collection.* $1200-1500

Single gun rig complete, with beautiful hand carved floral design, made by Charlie Baker. *Courtesy Paul and Marlene Snider.* $500-600

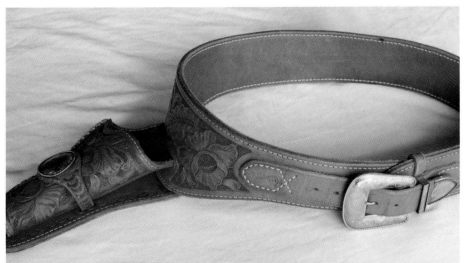

Charlie Baker is the maker of this single gun rig with sterling silver buckle and concho. The leather is "live oak" and tooled to perfection. *Courtesy Paul and Marlene Snider.* $650-750

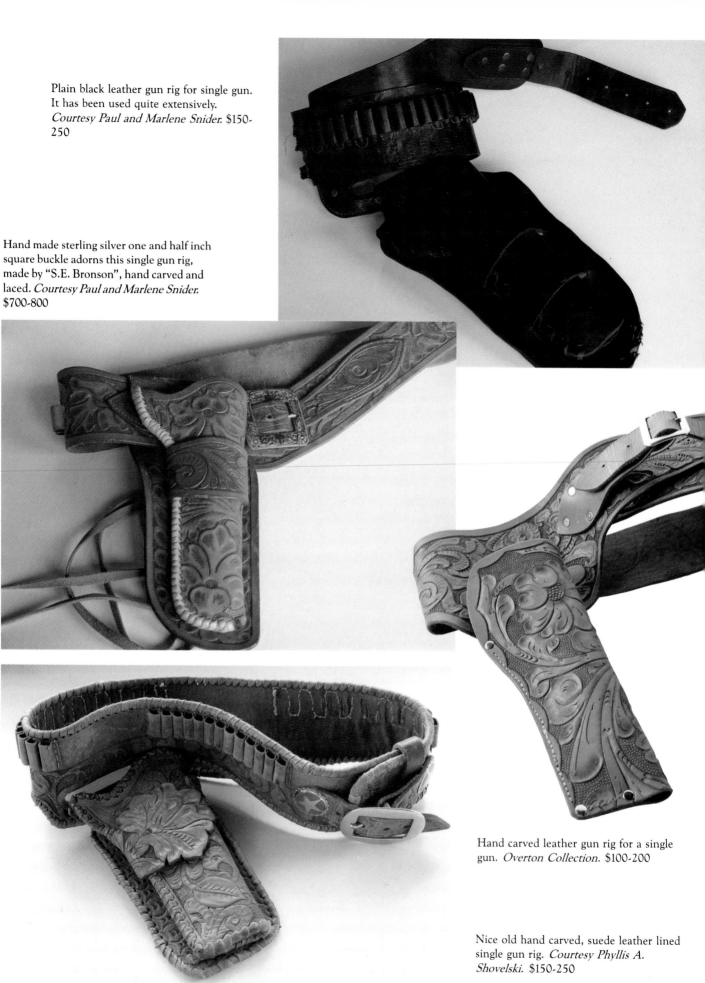

Plain black leather gun rig for single gun. It has been used quite extensively. *Courtesy Paul and Marlene Snider.* $150-250

Hand made sterling silver one and half inch square buckle adorns this single gun rig, made by "S.E. Bronson", hand carved and laced. *Courtesy Paul and Marlene Snider.* $700-800

Hand carved leather gun rig for a single gun. *Overton Collection.* $100-200

Nice old hand carved, suede leather lined single gun rig. *Courtesy Phyllis A. Shovelski.* $150-250

Very nice old double gun rig for two pistols, it is double buckled with sterling silver buckles. *Overton Collection.* $350-450

Single gun holster made in Portland, Oregon, they were used by early Plains detectives and officers. *Overton Collection.* $150-200

Rifle scabbard supported in a Native American beaded "squaw saddle", a very rare pairing of fine workmanship. *Courtesy Paul and Marlene Snider.* Saddle, $4000-6000; scabbard, $800-1200

Rifle scabbard made by Native Americans, beaded and fringed white "Buckskin". *Courtesy Paul and Marlene Snider.* $800-1200

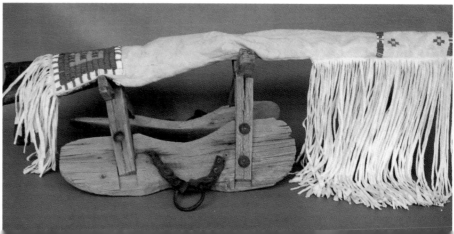

Winchester carbine 1866, it is a .44-40 and has been beautifully engraved on the brass sections. One of the most ornate carbines in existence. The engraving work done by the Late Great Charlie Baker. *Courtesy of Paul and Marlene Snider.* $7000-10000

Detail of ornate engraving on the Winchester 1866, shown on its side. *Courtesy Paul and Marlene Snider.*

The other side of the Winchester 1866. *Courtesy Paul and Marlene Snider.*

Detail of the engraving on the butt end of the Winchester 1866. *Courtesy Paul and Marlene Snider.*

Another popular saddle gun was the .25-.20 Winchester lever action. Sometimes the smaller caliber rifles were used by ranch women and youngsters, deemed more sensible for a woman or child because of the lesser "kick" to them.

Collectors of Western memorabilia also find gun rigs (holster with belt) rifle scabbards, belt knives, and pocket knives very attractive. They are all so representative of the cowboy life because these were the things that meant life and death to him. They were the "tools of his trade," just as sure as his saddle, bridle, boots, and spurs were to him, for what use were the other things if his gun or knife happened to fail him in a tight spot? While they may not have been used daily as were his other "tools," when he did happen to need them, he sometimes needed them desperately. It seems only proper and expected then, that both his gun and his knife were quite often taken care of by being kept in a leather holster or scabbard for their protection and safe keeping. Those items were often times decorative things in themselves, quite personalized and individualized by their makers and users.

Winchester .22 caliber single shot it is a bolt action, and generally given to a child or a lady. It is a Model 1904. *Overton Collection.* $850-1000

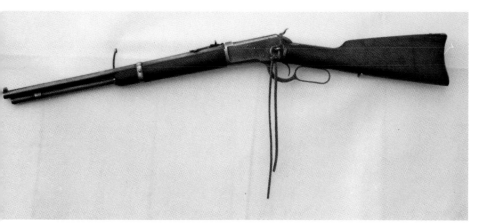

Winchester carbine, it is a .25-20 caliber, with Military butt and saddle ring. A very good example of what most range cowboys preferred to carry. *Overton Collection.* $700-900

Winchester .30 caliber carbine with a saddle ring. It is another rifle that was preferred by cowboys for a saddle gun. *Overton Collection.* $750-900

Winchester .30-30 caliber carbine made an excellent saddle gun, and believe me folks, it still does! *Overton Collection.* $500-700

Winchester .22 special with octagon barrel, it breaks down with a pistol grip. It is a Model 1890. *Overton Collection.* $850-1000

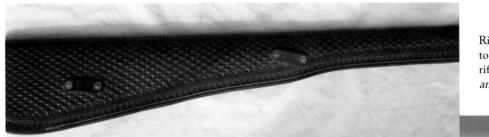

Rifle scabbard has been hand made and tooled with a basket weave design. Good rifles deserved good care. *Courtesy Paul and Marlene Snider.* $350-400

Very nice old rifle scabbard which was hand made, tooled, and laced. *Overton Collection.* $350-450

The top rifle scabbard is made of oil tanned "harness" leather, and is very old, the bottom is made of buffalo hide and is even older. *Overton Collection.* $500 each

Knife has four rivets in the bone handle, sheath made in saddle shop. *Overton Collection.* $25-45

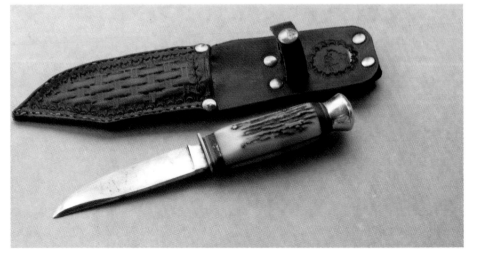

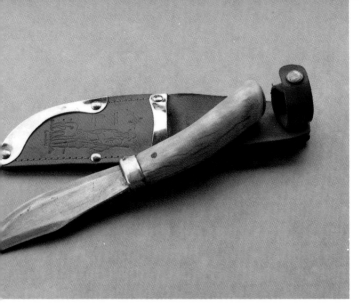

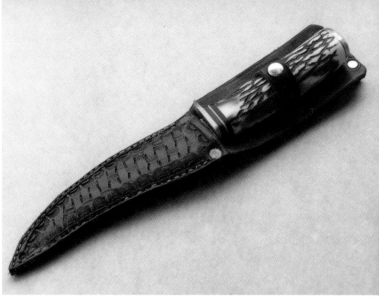

Hand made blade and horn handled with a piece of turquoise in end of handle, sheath probably a later pairing. *Overton Collection.* $45-65

This belt knife was termed the "Golden Spike", it is in a hand tooled sheath. *Overton Collection.* $45-60

Old camp belt knife and sheath, often carried by men in the saddle. *Overton Collection.* $50-60

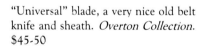

"Universal" blade, a very nice old belt knife and sheath. *Overton Collection.* $45-50

Belt knife called a "Case Boner", in a plain leather sheath. *Overton Collection.* $40-45

Western four and one half inch long all together, it was called a "Toothpick". *Overton Collection.* $40-50

Hand made belt knife with elk antler handle and hand made sheath. *Overton Collection.* $50-55

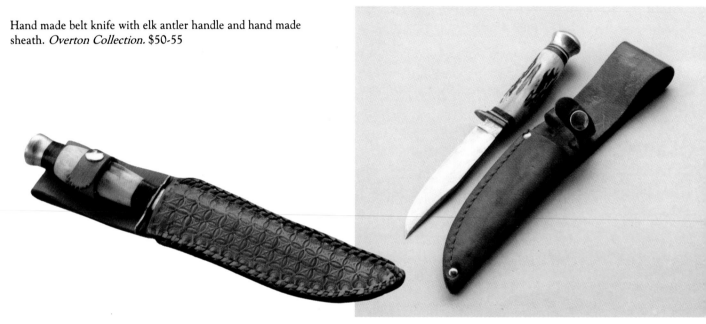

Home made knife and sheath with a deer antler handle and carbon steel blade. *Overton Collection.* $55-75

"Kinfolk" belt knife with a "Universal" steel blade. (Most all available belt knives today are made of stainless steel which cannot be sharpened and hold its edge like the old carbon steel blades did.) Handle is antler, finely polished and fitted. *Overton Collection.* $75-80

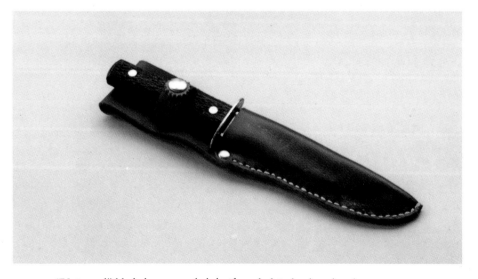

"Universal" bladed common belt knife and plain leather sheath. *Overton Collection.* $35-40

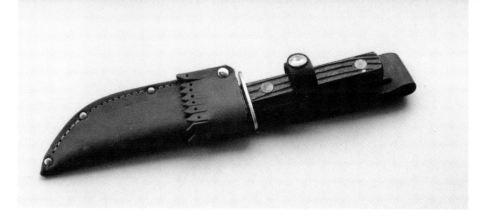

Common belt knife with a fringed leather sheath. *Overton Collection.* $35-40

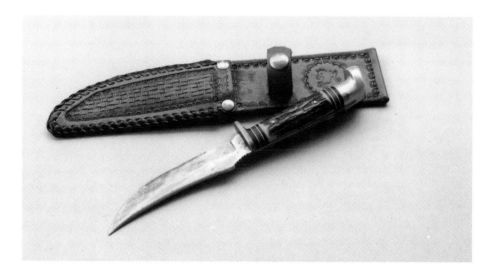

"Western" bone handled "Skinning" knife, carried in a hand made sheath, probably saddlemaker made. *Overton Collection.* $55-60

"Remington" belt knife with hand tooled sheath. *Overton Collection.* $55-65

"Buck" belt knife "Boner", it has a hand tooled and laced leather sheath. *Overton Collection.* $45-50

"K-Bar" common belt knife with very old plain leather sheath. *Overton Collection.* $50-60

"Kinfolk" belt knife with hand tooled sheath. *Overton Collection.* $55-65

Slim, very usable, all around type belt knife, with hand made sheath. *Overton Collection.* $75-80

"Kinfolk" belt knife with plain leather sheath. *Overton Collection.* $45-50

Common belt knife with leather sheath, knife has seen a lot of use, indicated on carbon steel blade. *Overton Collection.* $35-30

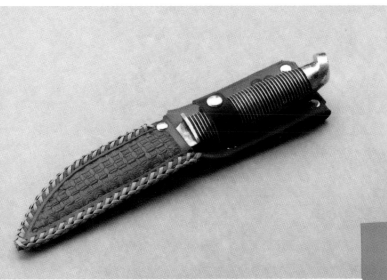

Fine boning knife with a splendid hand tooled, and laced leather sheath. *Overton Collection.* $25-40

Two very early but typical pocket knives carried quite often by trail hands, c. 1900. *Overton Collection.* $25-35 each

"Solengen" boot knife, with a hand tooled leather sheath. *Overton Collection.* $100-110

Old "Barlow" pocket knife c. 1915. *Overton Collection.* $35-45

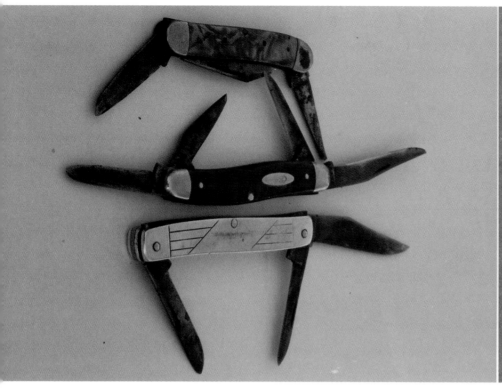

All three pocket knives are c. 1940s.
Overton Collection. $20-50 each

Left is a "Case"; Middle, "Schrade"; and
Right, "Boker"; all common trail and
ranch use pocket knives. *Overton
Collection.* $45-60

Three early pocket knives typical of rail
and ranch use. *Overton Collection.* $25-
35 each

Three old "Case" knives very well used
and typical of cowboy use. *Overton
Collection.* $35-45 each

Group of three standard pocket knives,
the one on the right has a bone handle.
Overton Collection. $45 each

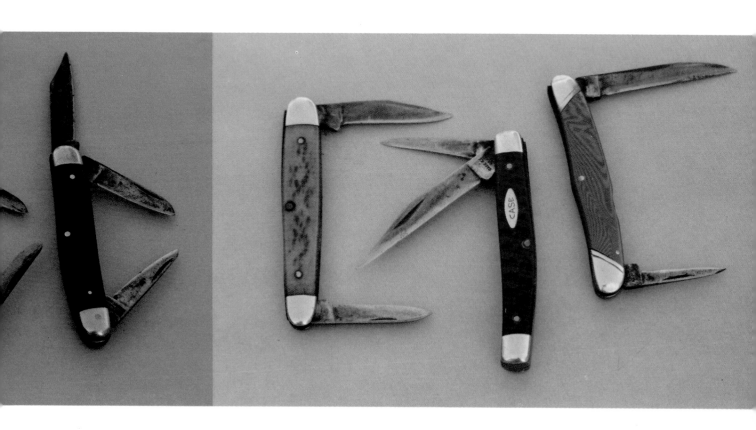

Left is a "Boker"; Middle knife, a "Case";
Right, "Hen and Chickens". *Overton
Collection.* Left, $25; Middle,$35; Right,
$60

CHAPTER NINE
CUFFS AND GAUNTLETS

Single cuff with a star design. As is the case with single spurs, one always hopes to find its mate. *Courtesy Marlin Pool.* $25-50

Leather cuffs were quite an asset to the working cowboy, for they served more than one purpose. They saved his arms from rope burns and brush, kept his shirt sleeves from wearing out so soon (the cuffs on a shirt were always the first thing to wear out), and were an attractive addition to his apparel and overall appearance. Because of the fact a new shirt was sometimes difficult to procure, or afford, the leather cuffs were a one time investment for a lifetime of shirt sleeve and arm protection.

Much as the present day cowboy wears his large silver belt buckle today, simply because it is the "in thing" to do, so also did the cowboy of yesteryear wear his decorative leather cuffs. Generally six to seven inches in length, the more "studded" or decorated they were, the better dressed he was. Today it is that same rule for the avid collector of cuffs, the more ornately studded they are, the higher the value most often.

On the other hand (no pun intended), there was the full gauntlet type gloves with wide cuffs that were also widely used by the cowboy, and now collected.

Most of the early gauntlets and gloves were made of soft deer skin. They had an unequaled feel on a man's hands and were greatly appreciated for protection, besides being decorative and attractive. Almost all of them were made and sold by the Native Americans. Sometimes a cowboy purchased them at a very nominal price, other times he might pay half a month's salary for a good pair that he particularly wanted.

Most gauntlets were lined with cotton calico or plain silk or cotton, and decorated with lovely colorful seed beads. Back then, a cowboy paid little attention to which tribe or Nation had made his gloves. Today, this is not only considered important to collectors, but also sometimes raises their value.

Gauntlets are a treasured item that is difficult to find outside a Museum. Very few have survived the passing of time, and the hard, sometimes destructive usage they were subjected to.

Fancy gauntlets, all beaded and fringed, were a favorite of the stars in the early Wild West Shows. Sometimes the early rodeo contestants also wore them. One of the most famous Western rodeo contestants of all time, "Jackson Sundown," an Native American cowboy, always wore them. One pair of his is included in the photos of this chapter. They are considered priceless.

Jackson Sundown was a Nez Perce who worked the early day rodeos. Some of his rides have become legendary. In 1916, at the age of fifty, Sundown captured the World Champion Bronc Riding title. These particular gloves or gauntlets were made by Jackson Sundown's wife. It is very unusual that the gloves have survived, and even more so that the written history and provenance has survived with them.

Matched pair of brass studded cuffs, c. 1920. *Courtesy Marlin Pool.* $100-125

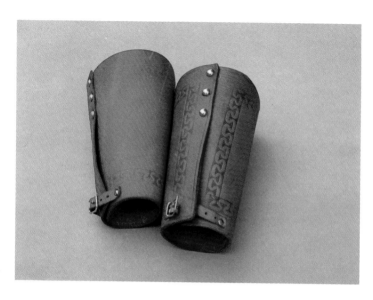

Pair of cuffs, considered Lady Cuffs because of the smaller size. *Courtesy Larry and Aileen Fisher.* $175-200

Pair of "FNO" studded cuffs. *Courtesy Larry and Aileen Fisher.* $275-350

Pair of very well used lace up cuffs. *Courtesy Paul and Marlene Snider.* $200-300

Native American beaded tie on cuffs, attributed to Yakima or Nez Perce. *Courtesy Larry and Aileen Fisher.* $325-450

Very rare and hard to find pair of child's cuffs, stamped leather with single snap. *Courtesy Paul and Marlene Snider.* $150-200

Desert rose stamped design on the borders. *Courtesy Paul and Marlene Snider.* $200-300

Diamond shape studs, the cuffs are smooth dark leather, and I am sure, have been well used. *Courtesy Paul and Marlene Snider.* $500-600

Star pattern and stamped design, they have a little added "roll" at the wear edge. *Courtesy Paul and Marlene Snider.* $600-700

The brass studs make up a large horseshoe design. *Courtesy Paul and Marlene Snider.* $450-550

Big star design in brass with a large brass concho in center. *Courtesy Paul and Marlene Snider.* $600-700

Horseshoe with brass studs and an unusual way of closing. *Courtesy Paul and Marlene Snider.* $450-550

Cuffs are marked "Buck Knapp, Maker Helena, Montana". *Courtesy Paul and Marlene Snider.* $300-400

Rose pattern with stars and nickel studs. *Courtesy Paul and Marlene Snider.* $300-400

Unique brass oval shaped studs in a daisy design. They are most unusual and ornate. *Courtesy Paul and Marlene Snider.* $750-900

Marked "Heiser, Denver" they are in pristine condition. *Courtesy Paul and Marlene Snider.* $500-600

Native American beaded gauntlets, attributed to the Nez Perce Nation. *Courtesy Larry and Aileen Fisher.* $450-550

Black bear hair winter type gauntlets, generally used by stage coach drivers, c. 1910. *Courtesy Paul and Marlene Snider.* $350-450

Deerskin and silver tip beaver, made by Fort Hall Shoshone, or Blackfoot Nation, c. 1920. *Courtesy Paul and Marlene Snider.* $800-1000

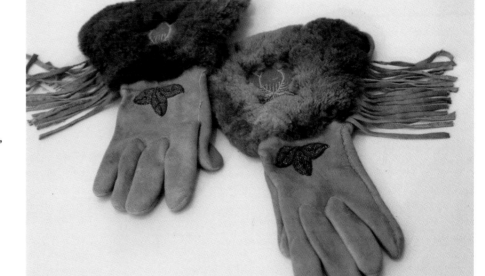

These gauntlets have a history provenance: "These gloves were given to me by Jackson Sundown, 1912. His wife did the work. signed Tommy High". Jackson Sundown was a very famous Native American rodeo contender in the early part of this century. He was World Champion Bronc Rider in 1916. *Courtesy Paul and Marlene Snider.* $1200-1500

Yakima Nation beadwork, deerskin with red rose pattern, c. 1870s-1880s. *Courtesy Paul and Marlene Snider.* $900-1000

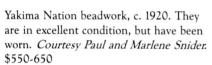

Yakima Nation beadwork, c. 1920. They are in excellent condition, but have been worn. *Courtesy Paul and Marlene Snider.* $550-650

Ojibwa Nation in the Great Lakes region beaded, they show use, but are in great condition, c. 1920s. *Courtesy Paul and Marlene Snider.* $350-425

Yakima Nation beaded Gauntlets, they are full beaded cuff style, somewhat rare to find because the tiny seed beads are so time consuming. *Courtesy Paul and Marlene Snider.* $650-750

Deerskin tanned men's gloves, they have built a lot of fence and roped a lot of cows. *Overton Collection.* $35-45

These are deerskin ladies gloves made by Native Americans, belonging to Judy Bertsch, a true cowgirl. *Courtesy Bob and Judy Bertsch.* $35-45

CHAPTER TEN
CLOTHING AND ACCESSORIES

"Look at a man's feet and look at his head, and its easy to tell what's in between."

Thomas Harvey Overton 1890-1982

Sometime during the 19th century the Mayor of Dodge City, a Mr. Robert Wright, observed that cowboys "delight in appearing rougher than they are." I wonder if that quote may not still be applicable for today.

It is only natural that the apparel of the cowboy has always varied greatly according to personal choice and preference. However, there were standards that even centuries ago seem to fit a common "mold." Many items were found to be necessary no matter which shape or color they might take.

A good beaver felt hat, for instance, was a vital piece of apparel. The logo inside the Stetson hats portrayed a cowboy bending down with his hat filled with drinking water offering it to his horse, indicating early on that a good hat could even be used for a bucket! His hat always seemed to "age" with him, and strangely enough, took on a kind of "personality" of its own, often reflecting a cowboy's own personality.

The everyday hat was broad brimmed and generally high crowned, but once in a while, sometimes even on a whim or a bet, the cowboy would buy himself a "Sunday-go-to-meeting" hat. These were usually in the shape of a "bowler" or "Homberg."

A good pair of leather boots was also necessary and the high heel and pointed toe were worn for a reason. The heels served two purposes, they kept the foot from slipping straight on through the stirrup, and they made a kind of seat for his spurs. The toe on the boot made it easy for a mans foot to "pick up" the stirrup when mounting, and easy to leave the stirrup even in an emergency. Being dragged by a horse with a "hung foot" was the kind of nightmare that no cowboy wanted to experience! Mr. Overton would never let me ride in my moccasins, because of the danger of a "hung foot" in the stirrups. (Remember, Native American saddles had no stirrups.)

A good jacket was also essential to a cowboy. While many were heavy wool flannel and later denim, there were very many that were made of buckskin. Like the gloves or gauntlets he may have used, his jacket quite often was purchased from the Native Americans and were therefore quite often decorated with beadwork.

Leather apparel of any kind has a way of surviving years of use and is often easier to find today than some of the other items and materials. Leather belts and good silver buckles are considered quite collectible today. The Ranger style of belt buckle, popular for so long, is very collectible. They quite often are decorated with gold and jewels on top of sterling silver. Some of the trophy style buckles are also becoming very desirable to collect, and they often carry the date it was won by the cowboy. They generally depict the rodeo event he had participated in.

A cowboy's neckerchief was also a very decorative useful item of apparel. Ordinarily they were made of common cotton calico, but sometimes a few good silk ones were purchased and worn. The neckerchiefs kept dust out of his nose and throat when pulled up "robbery style" and worn during the dusty trail rides as cattle herds kicked up dust and the trail hand stayed close with his herd. The cowboy riding "drag" especially found need for the neckerchief mask, as he was assigned last position behind the herd.

In later years, there has been a new surge of interest in early neckerchief collecting. The silk ones with any cowboy image seem to be most popular and collectible. They are generally found with bright, pure, colors, and sometimes portray rodeos of the West, such as the Pendleton Roundup, which has been in existence since 1910 and is still functioning in its original town of Pendleton, Oregon, every year in September.

Child's deerskin vest with studs and conchos, marked "Keyston Bros. Mfgrs. San Fran. Ca." also marked "Lasso Em Bill" c. 1930. *Courtesy Larry and Aileen Fisher.* $75-125

Hand constructed deerskin jacket, very old. *Courtesy Paul and Marlene Snider.* $1500-2000

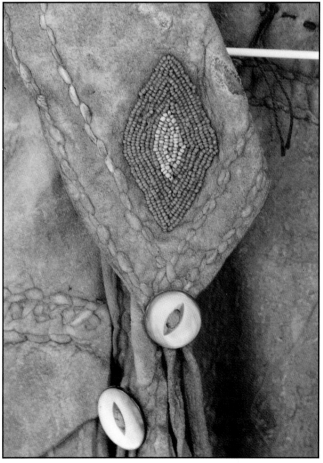

Beaded jacket with mother-of-pearl buttons, very old and hand constructed of deerskin. *Courtesy Paul and Marlene Snider.* $1500-2000

Detail of beadwork and mother-of-pearl buttons on jacket.

Native American deerskin beaded jacket, made by Umatillas.
Courtesy Paul and Marlene Snider. $2500

Back of previous jacket.

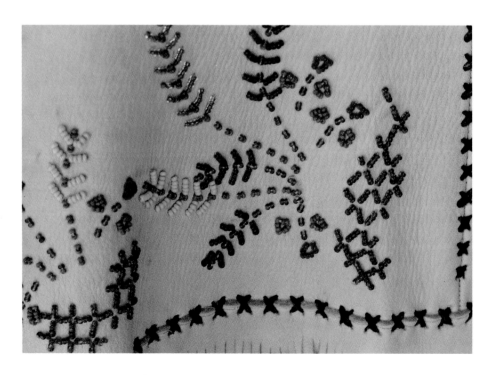

Detail of previous jacket.

Nez Perce beaded vest with cloth lining. *Courtesy Paul and Marlene Snider.* $1500-2000

Back side of Nez Perce vest.

Detail of beading on Nez Perce vest.

Very lovely Ogallala Sioux fully beaded vest, representing many long hours of labor. *Courtesy Paul and Marlene Snider.* $3500-5000

Back side of Ogallala Sioux vest.

Native American beaded deerskin vest with eagle motif. *Courtesy Paul and Marlene Snider.* $350-450

Back side of eagle vest.

Detail of eagle.

Canadian Indian beaded vest, constructed of moose hide. *Courtesy Paul and Marlene Snider.* $500-700

Back side of the moose hide vest.

Detail of beading on moose hide vest.

Canadian Indian beaded vest with tie front. *Courtesy Paul and Marlene Snider.* $500-700

Back side of Canadian Indian vest.

Very old beaded buckskin jacket, with contrast fringe. Excellent condition. *Courtesy Paul and Marlene Snider.* $600-700

Back view of white buckskin jacket.

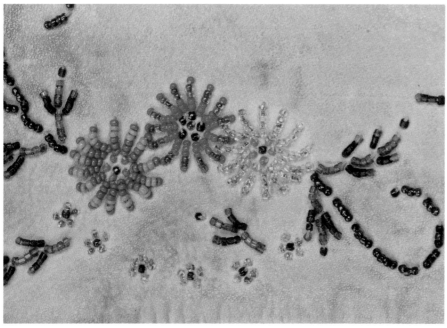

Detail photo of beading on white buckskin jacket.

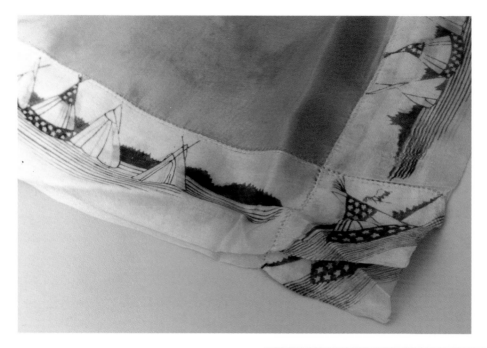

The border is actually considered an important factor when collecting old neckerchiefs. The neckerchiefs shown in this section are all pure silk. *Courtesy Larry and Aileen Fisher.* $75-225

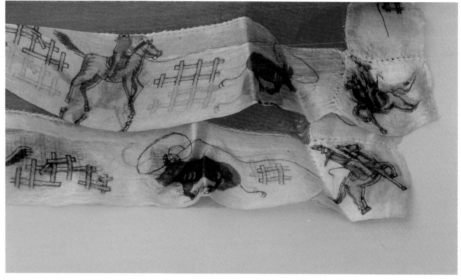

Borders that are especially "traditional cowboy" or are very decorative are always valuable. *Courtesy Larry and Aileen Fisher.* $75-225

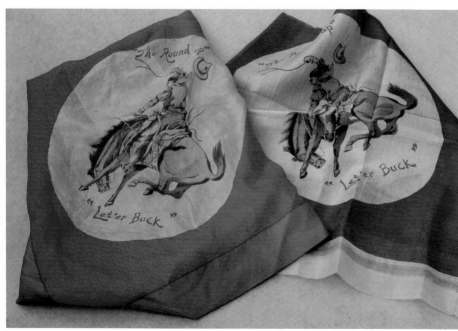

Neckerchief on right is dated "1-29-24" the one on the left is undated. *Courtesy Larry and Aileen Fisher.* $75-225 each

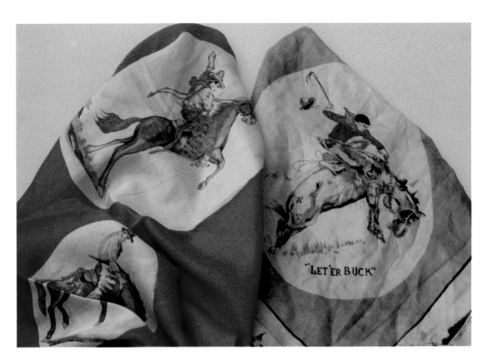

Red and green are always desirable colors. *Courtesy Larry and Aileen Fisher.* $75-225

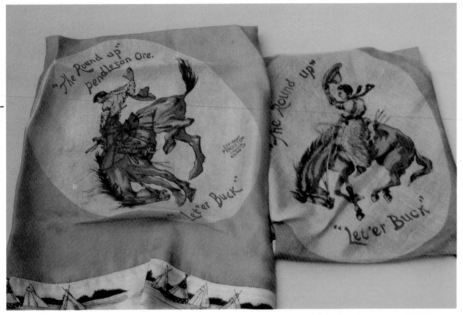

Neckerchief on the left has "Copyright Pendleton, Oregon Round Up", the one on right is unmarked. *Courtesy Larry and Aileen Fisher.* $75-225

A red and green "Let er Buck" neckerchief. *Courtesy Larry and Aileen Fisher.* $75-225

Green and red "Let er Buck" neckerchief. *Courtesy Larry and Aileen Fisher.* $75-225

Both are very early silk neckerchiefs. *Courtesy Larry and Aileen Fisher.* $75-225

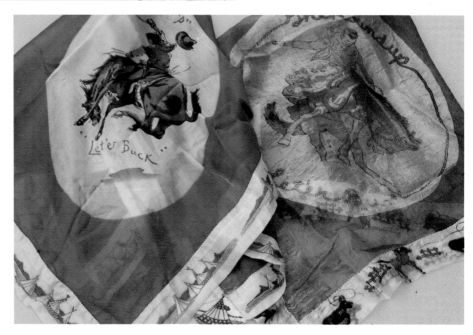

Blue neckerchiefs with intricate borders. *Courtesy Larry and Aileen Fisher.* $75-225

Unusual "bull-on-the-range" motif on
this silk neckerchief. *Courtesy Larry and
Aileen Fisher.* $75-225

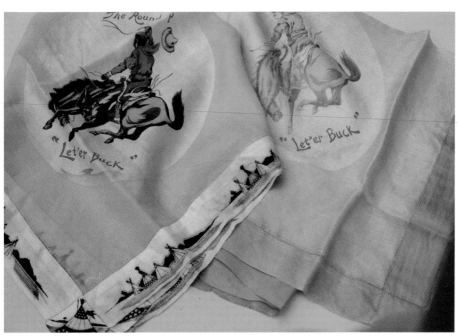

Neckerchief on the left is probably higher
value than the one on the right. Both are
very nice silk neckerchiefs. *Courtesy Larry
and Aileen Fisher.* $75-225

Lovely design and border on this silk
neckerchief. *Courtesy Larry and Aileen
Fisher.* $75-225

Very early trophy type belt buckle done in gold and silver. *Overton Collection.* $150-200

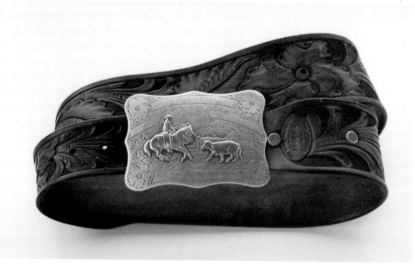

Early old trophy style belt buckle and belt. They were oftentimes donated to the events by some of the local storekeeps or merchants. *Overton Collection.* $250-300

Detail of saddlemakers mark on belt.

Gold and silver belt buckles that are considered "genuine", in other words, truly "earned" in some event, and then used a very long time by the man himself...are very collectible, but beware of many fakes. This was won by Mr. Overton thirty two years ago and is still being worn. *Overton Collection.* $200-300

It is very unusual to find a pure copper trophy belt buckle. This one is c. 1940s *Overton Collection.* $75-100

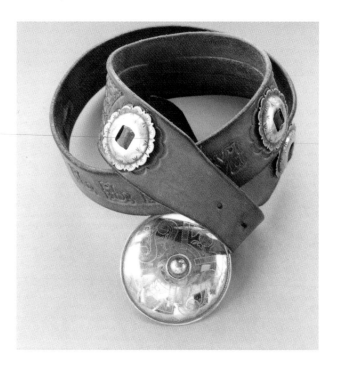

Very unusual round silver buckle decorated with engraving. The conchos on belt are Visalia. *Overton Collection.* $350-450

Hand tooled little ladies' belt and silver buckle set, it was given to the young Judy Stirewalt when she was only a few years old. Judy rode the Stirewalt range working with the regular cowhands all of her young life. *Courtesy Bob and Judy Bertsch.* $75-100

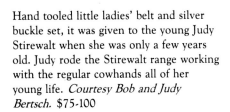

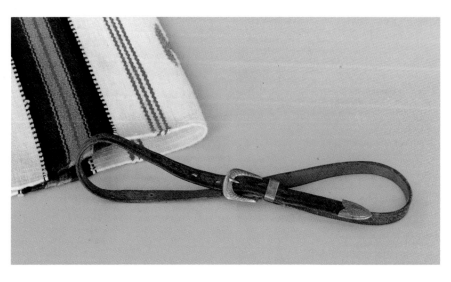

All three of these belt buckles are done in the old traditional "ranger" style which is becoming very collectible lately. They were almost always done in pure silver and sometimes with fancy gold overlays and jewels. *Overton Collection.* $350-550 each

Ranger belt buckle and belt, the buckle set is adorned with rose gold. *Overton Collection.* $900-1200

Ranger buckle set, it is covered with engraved rose gold and silver. *Overton Collection.* $900-1200

Ranger buckle set decorated with rose gold on top of sterling silver. *Overton Collection.* $900-1200

Sunburst design on sterling silver, this ranger buckle set is a unique design. *Overton Collection.* $350-550

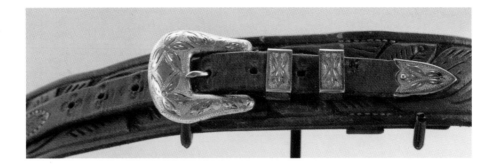

Ranger style buckle with sterling silver and gold overlays. *Overton Collection.* $750-900

Plain leather "buckaroo belt", these were used by the early day cowboys who participated in rodeo, they acted as "back protector" when on the bucking stock. *Courtesy Larry and Aileen Fisher.* $150-175

Decorative studded "buckaroo belt". *Courtesy Larry and Aileen Fisher.* $225-275

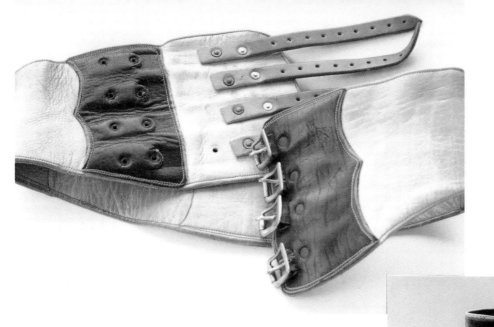

Early buckle type "buckaroo belt" done in two shades of smooth leather. *Overton Collection.* $225-300

Old "Paul Bond" boots with quilted tops, antique silver spurs. Boots are c. 1940 *Overton Collection.* Boots only $350-450

The boots are "Paul Bond" with old August Buermann spurs with star rowels. Jack Williams in the photo with spurs on, photo of him on horse was taken in 1919, in Rosebud County, Montana. *Courtesy Roy and Jeanenne Williams.* Spurs $800-900

Boots and old Buermann spurs in photo of Jack Williams in 1919. *Courtesy Roy and Jeanenne Williams.* $800-900

"Blucher" boots with old style square toe, and spurs from Mexico silver mounted and well made. *Courtesy Roy and Jeanenne Williams.* $500-600

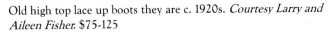

Old high top lace up boots they are c. 1920s. *Courtesy Larry and Aileen Fisher.* $75-125

Pair of contemporary decorative painted boots with spurs. *Courtesy Larry and Aileen Fisher.* $75-100

This is typical of cowboy Stetson marked with XXXX inside crown of hat, it also reads "Jack Wolf Ranchwear" c. 1940s *Courtesy Phyllis A. Shovelski.* $100

"Beaver Hat Co." marked with five XXXXX inside the crown. On any of the beaver felt cowboy hats, the more Xs inside the crown, the better the quality. This one still bears blood stains from a very bad "bull wreck" the cowboy injured when the bull took him up into the grandstands many years ago. *Overton Collection.* $100

This is a classic style popular with cowboys who wanted a real "Sunday-Go-To-Meetin" hat. It is a "Resistol" "Self Conforming, and Kitten Finish", a very nice old Homburg with its original hat box. *Overton Collection.* $175-250

CHAPTER ELEVEN
DESK COLLECTIBLES

There is something to be said for collecting the smaller things that remind us of the cowboy's world, and yet require very little room to display and enjoy. Since we can't all be saddle collectors, there are numerous items just as attractive and desirable that make up a category I call "Desk Collectibles." These things are an attractive addition sitting on a desk or coffee table as conversation pieces, or just because in some small way they speak of the cowboy and are pleasant for us to behold.

Each of us have our own reasons for liking what we like, and collecting what we do. Because "variety is the spice of life," it quite naturally varies greatly with each one of us. Included in this final chapter are some items that I found in people's "Treasures." Some may or may not have been used by a working cowboy or Ranch owner, but still fall into that group of unique collectible and cowboy related.

In the final analysis, who is to say what mattered the most to that worn and weary trail hand who had perhaps not slept, eaten, or shaved recently? Was there a moment when his silverware counted more than his saddle? While it may seem far fetched, life has a way of serving up surprises and strange kinds of circumstances and I am very certain that is just what it often did in the life of the man who made his living in the saddle and out on the cow trails.

In any case, I hope you will enjoy seeing a few of these small items that complete the list for all of the "wonderful things" that I have looked upon as "Treasure."

Horse without the saddle.

Bronze horse with an unique removable saddle. These bronze horses were so popular in the forties and fifties almost every home had one on the mantle. Today they are very scarce and very collectible. This is an unusual type as very few were made with saddles that came off. *Courtesy Larry and Aileen Fisher.* $250-325

Rearing horses have always been popular and especially if they are made of some desirable material such as carved wood, alabaster, or ivory. (Thank You My Tuffy for this one). *Overton Collection.* $250-325

Miniature working mechanisms, these tiny guns have a very real "feel" to them. The revolvers break open, the cylinder actually revolves, the lever breaks open on the carbine and its hammer comes back, etc. Toys of the "grown" kids. *Overton Collection.* $50 each

Miniatures have always found a good home or desk to recline upon. This tiny saddle has a real saddle tree in it just as do the full sized ones, and took almost as long to build by a Journeyman Saddlemaker. *Overton Collection.* $250-350

Salesman samples are always desirable as they tell us today, in miniature, what was available yesterday. This is a salesman sample of hat and box available quite a few years back. *Courtesy Larry and Aileen Fisher.* $45-65

Authentic as to detail, the little wagons of yesteryear are very collectible. *Overton Collection.* $75-125

Tiny stagecoach, correct in detail, the doors open and the "boot" where luggage was stored is made of leather. *Overton Collection.* $75-125

An unfinished Peace Pipe, carved for us by a man named "Walking Bear" of Nez Perce nation, rests on an old metal saddle horn. *Overton Collection.* $200-300

Rancher wallet probably made by the local saddlemaker in town. The man's name was never tooled into the "ribbon". *Overton Collection.* $45-65

Rancher wallet, it has been hand carved and tooled in fine leather. Years ago, wallets like these were used instead of banks. *Overton Collection.* $45-75

Livestock tally book, made of hand carved leather and in excellent condition with original pages within. *Overton Collection.* $45-75

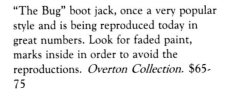

Boot jacks, used by the cowboy to easily remove his boots after a hard day's work. The one on the right reads: "Property of Wells Fargo Express, San Francisco Division" *Overton Collection.* $55 left, $255 right

"The Bug" boot jack, once a very popular style and is being reproduced today in great numbers. Look for faded paint, marks inside in order to avoid the reproductions. *Overton Collection.* $65-75

While it may be true that the real cowboy never used ash trays for his "roll-your-own's," sometimes the ranch owner did. Ones like this were given away by travelling salesmen to promote their "Medicine Wagon Wares". *Overton Collection.* $45-55

Old horse grooming brush, it is leather topped and listed in the 1902 Sears Roebuck Catalog. *Courtesy Marlin Pool.* $50-75

Both brushes are from the 19th century, the one on left is walnut wood with sterling silver ornamentation, and the one on the right is capped with engraved sterling silver. Used by the well groomed cowboy on a Saturday night, if he was lucky. *Overton Collection.* $75-175

Shaving kit for the ranch owner, it is doubtful that many trail hands had anything so fine in their bunk house. There is a lady in her bonnet pictured. *Overton Collection.* $700-1200

Inside the 19th century shaving kit. The brush has a carved genuine ivory handle, and the razor is also ivory.

Leather box made for a man's personal items. It is marked "Hamley and Co." and so was made in a saddle shop in Pendleton, Oregon, c. 1930s. *Courtesy Larry and Aileen Fisher.* $60-100

Decorative horse brass, hung on the harness and sometimes told who the owners were and what trade they may have been into. The one on the bottom is a pony-cart brass. *Overton Collection.* $55-75 each

Patriotic colors were often used for harness spreaders, these are in pristine condition. *Overton Collection.* $75-125

Five ranger buckle sets, all sterling silver. *Overton Collection.* $350-950 each

Horse head rosettes, they are glass topped and are very scarce items, some are being reproduced today. One can examine the backs to tell if they are old and genuine. The very badly bent belt buckle standing on edge on the right in photo was a result from a lucky (or not) horse kick to the man's middle. *Courtesy Bob and Judy Bertsch.* $125-150

Set of matching sterling silver conchos. Often used on saddles and bridles. *Overton Collection.* $250-350

Genuine U.S. Cavalry brass bridle buttons with loops on the back, difficult to find in any condition. *Overton Collection.* $200

The standard eating utensils for a cowboy. *Overton Collection.* $45-65

Bone handled silverware, standard for the times. *Overton Collection.* $45-75

Complete set, with bone handles and sheath for extra knife. *Overton Collection.* $45-75

BIBLIOGRAPHY

Listed here are the writings I have found useful in the making of this book. It is by no means a complete record of all the sources I have consulted, but is listed as a suggestion for further reading.

Arnold, Oren. *Roundup of Western Literature.* Banks Upshaw and Company, 1949.

Ault, Phillip H. *The Home Book of Western Humor.* New York: Dodd, Mead and Company, 1967.

Babcock, Gil, and Bud Hildenbrand. *Bridle Bits of the West.* Printed by Creative Printing,1972.

Ball, Robert W.D. and Ed Vebell. *Cowboy Collectibles and Western Memorabilia.* Atglen, Pennsylvania: Schiffer Publishing Ltd., 1991.

Barker, S. Omar. *Songs of the Saddlemen.* Denver, Colorado: Sage Books, 1954.

Beatie, Russel H. *Saddles.* Oklahoma: University of Oklahoma Press, 1981.

Forbis, William H. *The Cowboys.* New York: Time Life Books, 1973.

Maul, Patrice, and Jack Ferguson with Mike and Gretchen Graham. *Canon City Spur, Colorado Prison Spurs, and The Men Who Made Them.* Canon City Spur Company and Old West Trading Compapny, 1995.

Nelson, Mark Loge. *Bibliography of Old Time Saddlemakers.* Nelson Publishing, Rt. 1, Box 220, Palouse, Washington 99161.

Pattie, Jane. *Cowboy Spurs and Their Makers.* Texas: Texas A&M University Press, 1991.

Pendlton, Oregon, Pioneer Ladies Club. *Reminiscences of Oregon Pioneers.* Pendleton, Oregon: East Oregonian Publishing Co., 1937.

Trachtman, Paul. *The Gunfighters.* New York: Time Life Books, 1974.

INDEX

IN CLOSING

"Their tales are told. Their book is closed. Never again will such a people go forward to populate a new earth. We, their children, bow in reverence."

from: *Reminiscences of Oregon Pioneers*

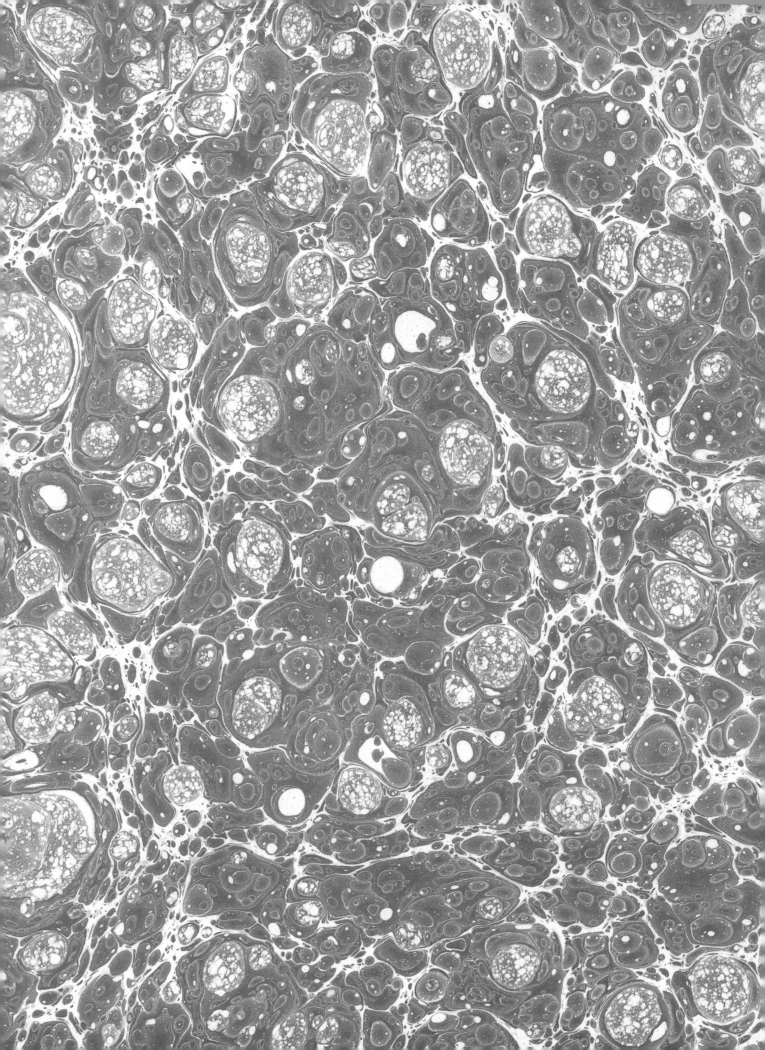